THE GIFT OF ENCOURAGEMENT

Living Powerfully Through Adversity

D1522518

JOHN J. DIETER

THE GIFT OF ENCOURAGEMENT

ISBN: 978-1-886296-45-9

Published in the United States by
Arrow Publications
P.O. Box 10102
Cedar Rapids, IA 52410
Telephone: (319)395-7833
Toll Free: (877) 363-6889 (U.S. only)
Fax: (319)395-7353
www.arrowbookstore.com

Cover design by Karen Goodell.
Interior design and photo layout by Emily Speight

ENDORSEMENTS

We all need encouragement in our life and the strength to overcome adversity. For myself I have found that primary source of encouragement and strength from God. But He also sends people into my life to encourage and strengthen me even more.

John Dieter is one such person who has blessed me, the Fellowship ministry, Israel, and the Jewish people. It is therefore appropriate that he write such a wonderful book on the spiritual roots of encouragement and strength in overcoming adversity. He has been a blessing to Israel and a devoted supporter of The International Fellowship of Christians and Jews. He demonstrates that commitment with the admirable goal to help airlift 2,000 Jews to their homeland in Israel. The adversity he overcame in his own life has given him immeasurable compassion and the zeal to make a difference in others' lives. I thank God for people like him.

(The International Fellowship of Christians and Jews fosters understanding and cooperation between Christians and Jews and builds broad support for Israel and other shared concerns.)

His Excellency Rabbi Yechiel Eckstein
A Goodwill Ambassador of the State of Israel

Advisor to the Prime Minister
Issues of Immigration and the Christian Community

President
International Fellowship of Christians and Jews
Chicago, IL

Your work in support of Israel is praiseworthy and noble. Thank you for standing with us, especially during these difficult times.

Warmest Regards,

His Excellency Daniel Ayalon
Ambassador of Israel
Washington, DC

Dedication
& Acknowledgements

This work of love is dedicated to my heavenly Father who knew me before the foundation of the universe and planned every step I would take, guiding along the journey. He places His mighty hand on my head and directs my path. I stand amazed at the places and people I have met, whether in Cedar Rapids, Israel, Washington, D.C., Kiev, or the Crimea. God plans each step I take, and as I humble myself under His direction, new worlds are opened to me.

I want to thank the Holy Spirit who helped me write this book. I thank my godly mother who trained her children to cheerfully serve God and who was a selfless example of faith and endurance in action. I thank those I love and the many who love me. For their loving care, encouragement, and wisdom in editing, I would also like to thank Lila Nelson, Kathy Croy, and Emily Speight. (Special thanks to Emily for the final edit and formatting, and for not letting me settle for second best.) I thank Karen Goodell for her thoughtful skill in designing the cover. I am so pleased with everyone whose effort and skill made this book possible! Thanks also to Tim and Linda Ferry who first shared that God told them I had a story to tell.

CONTENTS

Foreword..11

Introduction: Comfort, Comfort My People......................13

PART ONE: UNEXPECTED TRAGEDY

Chapter One: Dreams of Promise in a Foreign Land:
Entering the Unknown......................................23

Chapter Two: Nine/Nine/Eighty-one:
A Defining Moment that Tested My Character........31

Chapter Three: Greatly Bruised, Greatly Used:
Maturity During Hardship............................41

Chapter Four: Courage Under Fire: I Shall Not Die,
but Live to Tell of All His Deeds!..............49

PART TWO: RECOVERY

Chapter Five: The Promise:
Moses, God's Gift to Humanity....................69

Chapter Six: Beauty for Ashes:
The Road to Recovery Begins........................79

Chapter Seven: Recovering the Promise:
A Corporate Promotion at Eighty..............88

Chapter Eight: Days of Light, Moments of Hope:
Healing Your Memories.................................95

PART THREE: RESTORATION

Chapter Nine: Visions and Angels:

Spiritual Gifts to Encourage You.........................103

Chapter Ten: After the Rain, the Sun Begins to Shine:

Discovering Purpose After Tragedy.....................113

Chapter Eleven: Zev Kedem:

A Schindler Jew Celebrates Life!...........................121

Chapter Twelve: Days of Promise:

The Fulfillment of a Dream.................................127

Chapter Thirteen: Fellowship and Favor

The White House...136

FOREWORD

I have known John Dieter for a number of years. I have observed his life and have found him to be a yielded, giving vessel. He has gone through some very difficult situations in life. But through it all, with courage and faith, he has continued to press further into the calling the Lord has given him. John has survived tragic events, yet continues to maintain both his integrity and humor during adversity. Thus, he encourages others to persevere as well. Out of obedience and trust, John ventures to wherever the Lord leads him. He has received amazing favor from God with people from around the world and is the first to give all glory to the Lord.

Encouragement and overcoming adversity is truly a gift of the heart. John's purpose in writing this book is to be a faithful witness to what the Lord will do in anyone's life! He has a large visionary view of life and this gift has given him courage under fire.

Francis Frangipane
Author and Pastor

INTRODUCTION

COMFORT, COMFORT MY PEOPLE

The Gift of Encouragement is meant to be a comfort and a strategic tool for the weary of heart. It is for those who suddenly find themselves in a situation for which there seems to be no answer. In the moments of life that test your soul, it is important to stay focused on God's promises for your life. No matter what the circumstances look like, hold tightly to the promise of God's Word that your situation will get better. In the end, you will be placed in a higher position of restoration than before. Anything the enemy has taken from you will be restored sevenfold (See Ps. 71:20-21).

■ ■ ■

So what do you do when your life is catapulted into chaos? What happens when your life direction is changed almost instantaneously by a force or situation that you have no control over? What do you do when you've done everything right, but everything goes wrong?

What plan of action do you take to remedy the problems? Or do you choose to take no action? In those moments when there is nothing you can do to change the situation, what answers do you give others? How do you graciously address the complex issues and respond appropriately to the questions your loved ones pose?

The purpose of this book is to encourage and comfort people who are going through difficult times. It's to give them hope that things will get better. But there is only one way out of the quagmires that people get into: making the conscious choice to remain positive and look upward and outward. The only course of action is to keep your eyes focused on Jesus and remain "intensely focused" on others. As we do this, the Lord remains faithful, encouraging us; "I am leaving you with a gift—peace of mind and heart! And the peace I give isn't fragile like the peace the world gives. So don't be troubled or afraid" (John 14:27).

When our attention is focused on others, the problems we face become manageable. However, when we choose to turn our focus inward, the enemy uses this to pull us into deeper depths of despair. Making the decision to remain selflessly focused on others will save you much heartache.

I have chosen to write this book to be a light and encouragement to those who are in a stream of confusion about their life. The book is divided into three parts. Each part parallels my life, when a near-death experience instantly set my future in a direction not of my choosing. But, being faithful and diligent, God brought me through to the other side with great victory and restoration! He will do the same with your life! From my experiences, I know this. Trust Him! When God has a special promise for your life, don't give up on it. Be an encouragement to others when you are going through a difficult situation. It will be your saving grace. God will restore your life to a greater fullness than you could ever imagine! (See Job 42:10).

Hold firmly to the promise that God has personally given for your life, for your promise is unique and full of power! In due time, God will release you in the great anointing that He has intended for you since before the very creation of the earth. He has established this plan for you. Be encouraged! You are very special to the Father. He takes no pleasure when His precious child is hurting. His heart is also deeply grieved, and He feels your hurt!

This book is comprised of three parts:

PART ONE: Unexpected Tragedy. I will talk about the events that set our lives in directions we haven't planned. I will use the biblical example of Joseph being sold into Egypt. He did not want to go there, but in the place of being broken, he grew into a servant God could use greatly! I will also tell of being severely burned in an explosion that changed my life dramatically.

PART TWO: Recovery. I will discuss the journey to recovery from a catastrophic event and how to persevere. I will use the example of Israel's journey from bondage in Egypt to recovery of the Promised Land. Also, I will recount my long journey to recovery from an explosion that burned 68 percent of my body when I was nineteen years old.

PART THREE: Restoration. God will restore your life to a *better* condition than it was in the beginning, but it will take time and faith. I will use the example of King David and the restoration of Israel. I will also share about the amazing restorative miracles God has done in my life and His fulfillment of a promise He made to me when I was only twelve years old. This promise has led me to Israel and the White House, and it is only just beginning!

The Gift of Encouragement will give you the tools necessary to lift your eyes above the horizon and see the God we serve. He is always there with us, gently helping us, though we may feel abandoned at times. Even David came to this conclusion: "I spoke to hastily when I said, 'The Lord has deserted me,' for you listened to my plea and answered me" (Ps. 31:22). If a man after the very heart of God felt despair at times, maybe we should not be so harsh on ourselves when life makes no sense and all that we have faithfully worked for disappears.

This book should bring comfort to your heart as you read of the trials I have overcome through Christ and the triumphs I experienced after my life-altering experience.

There is always a special time and place for our hearts to be comforted by the eternal reach of our loving God. Our souls search passionately for the fulfillment of this great desire. We often experience an increased need to be comforted as a result of sudden loss or tragedy. During these unexpected events of tragic proportion, we are left reeling backwards, wondering what went wrong. We were faithful and diligent to our life plan, but suddenly an event seemed to abort our future, putting it into the uncertain galaxy of time and space. We are left wondering, *what did I do wrong to deserve this discomfort?* Often the answer is not so simple; the issues of life are complex. However, we know that with faith, all things are possible.

Often that is where we find ourselves, looking to the greatest power in heaven and earth, the power of God Almighty and the authority of His Anointed One, Jesus Christ! He promised to send the Comforter, who works through each believer. As He works through us, it is our responsibility to release this gift of encouragement by being a vessel that comforts others. That is so important to realize! God's promise is, "Fear not, for I am with you. Do not be dismayed. I am your God. I will strengthen you; I will help you; I will uphold you with my victorious right hand" (Isa. 41:10).

There have been times in my life when things just went wrong. As a person of faith, I knew that this was not part of God's ultimate plan for my life. Having prior knowledge of this gave me the courage to press into the open arms of God and know that, with time, everything would work out for the better.

In history there are many examples of people who encouraged and comforted those around them, even at great expense to themselves. When we get out of our selfish nature and operate in the realm of the selfless Christian, we become empowered with God's wisdom and ability to accelerate us through the situation.

Our main objective should be to bring comfort to the hurting child who lost a parent or kindness to the grieving spouse who suddenly found their world empty. At these times in life, we need to take extra precautions to be sensitive to the needs of those around us.

Recently, I was introduced to a man named Zev Kedem, a "Schindler Jew." I was fortunate to meet him at the University of Wisconsin at Platteville, where he gave a presentation to over two thousand people. His main theme was this: when he and his fellow captives faced hard, uncertain times in concentration camps, their love for each other kept them going. As the never-ending dread and terror in the work camps went on, this love and comfort gave each surviving soul the courage to face another day.

Meeting him was a great encouragement for me to continue being a vessel for God to use, making a difference in the world. If we think one person can't make a difference, we are wrong and have shortsighted assumptions. There are many examples of this in the Bible as well as in our society and neighborhoods. We just have to look carefully to see people who are making a great difference, right where they are in their daily lives! Just look in the mirror and you will see one who can be making a difference even now!

■ ■ ■

PRAYER OF ENCOURAGEMENT: *Father, God of love, light and restoration, lift up your people who are hurting. Enfold them in your radiant love, power and gentleness. I ask, Holy Spirit, for your presence and encouragement for those who are searching for answers and need the gifts the Comforter brings. Father, Holy God, I love you and ask this in Jesus' precious name. Heal the brokenhearted and open their eyes to the beauty of your presence! Give them the working knowledge of your revealed Word. Therein lies the answers for those in need of the healing touch of encouragement. Father, seal this in Jesus' blood and release your ministering angels to do their work, for they are servants of fire sent to perform your Word. Father, I speak this over your people now, in Jesus' name!*

PART ONE

UNEXPECTED TRAGEDY

How do you survive the unexpected tragedy that strikes with pale-white terror in your heart and life? That event could be an unforeseen divorce, the death of an immediate family member, or an accident. How do you recognize the truth of the emergency while not becoming bitter about the situation you've suddenly found yourself in?

What strength do you call on when your own has evaporated like the morning dew in the parched desert sun? How do you comprehend the complex possibilities of your future, yet not get discouraged?

These are difficult problems and questions. But the Lord is there with us, even when we don't feel Him. Have we been abandoned? Of course not! But we feel that we have been! Remember, God's Word assures us He will not abandon or forsake us.

Drawing close to the Lord during this strategic time is the best maneuver you can make as you start your recovery process. In time, you will recover from the challenge that has undermined your current abilities. But until then, the Lord will empower you with patience to run the good race and finish it, by His grace.

These are not just pretty words on a page. I have had to face and walk through these issues myself, finding the courage to be a much stronger individual. And you, too, will have your victory! You will have a resolute gentleness about your demeanor that emits God's radiant love. You will be restored!

■ ■ ■

CHAPTER ONE:

DREAMS OF PROMISE IN A FOREIGN LAND

Entering the Unknown

When I think of Joseph in his days of promise and hope, I wonder how he felt as he was sold into slavery, not knowing what his future would be.

■ ■ ■

It had been a beautiful morning. He awoke early, like he had done every day for seventeen years. He was full of life! He was bubbling with joy, full of amazement that God would use him with his newfound gift—dreams! Oh, to be young and full of aspiration and hope! There is nothing like it on earth!

As he awoke, he might have told his father how much he loved him. He knew that he was favored by his old but godly father as a product of the great love that Jacob had for Rachel.

Rachel had been the love of Jacob's life. Sadly, she died on 11 Cheshvan 2208 of the Jewish calendar, the day Benjamin was born. Joseph was only eight years old when his precious mother died. I can imagine his tears of sadness and grief as he stood by his mother's grave in the cave on the road to Bethlehem.

It would have been very difficult for Joseph. With questions of why and moments of tearful silence, he endured that inner loneliness that a child experiences when they lose a parent. Having almost lost my mother when I was eight years old, I understand this. It is difficult to make sense of changes, and children can deeply experience the uncertain feeling of disaster and loss.

Joseph might have witnessed the overwhelming grief of Jacob, inconsolable, as he said his last tender prayer for his beloved bride. *Rachel,* the one he had worked fourteen long years for, the one who had stirred his heart and passions! The youthful bride who had made those fourteen years seem like only a day. It was that tender, intimate love he desired, but now she had gone on to rest in the gentle hands of their eternal God. Jacob dearly loved the sons he had with Rachel, but especially Joseph, who was older and probably looked like her. Whenever Jacob looked into Joseph's sad and questioning eyes, he pondered the warm memories hidden in his heart; he was always reminded of her. She had been so beautiful, full of tender love and abandoned adventure!

It must have stirred Joseph's emotions to know that such a great love existed and that he was the son of a long awaited promise. To compensate for the loss of his mother, God had given Joseph a very special gift: *dreams!* This gift elevated young Joseph's imagination into the destiny God was preparing him for. I believe Joseph's father was tender toward him because of Joseph's willingness to be obedient and try to please his father. However, jealousy and resentment increased in the hearts of Joseph's ten older brothers.

It had to have been late in the season, when summer turns to fall, because the flocks were far from home; the upper highland pastures of Dothan were cooler than the desert during the last hot summer days. Jacob had asked Joseph to see how his brothers were doing as they tended the flocks.

Joseph bounced down the road toward his brothers, eating the apple in his hand. His innocent life was full of hope! Little did young Joseph realize that the events of that day would drastically change his future.

I wonder what he was thinking as he took that long walk to look for his brothers—his own brothers. Would Joseph have told them of his recent dream? You know, the one about his brothers—the one that might have been a source of encouragement to Reuben, Dan, Judah and the others?

Joseph confidently walked into the situation, not knowing that it would change his life forever. But seeing the look in his brothers' eyes, he knew there was trouble in the air! Sure, he knew they were jealous of him, but he did not realize to what extent until their plan unfolded.

Joseph's limp body slammed to the bottom of the dry well. Who knows how deep it was? Thirty feet? Fifty feet? Only Joseph knew the depths of his despair as he fell helplessly into the plan that was meant to kill him. This innocent youth's life changed in an instant, and he had no control.

I wonder how Joseph felt, sitting shocked and dazed in the bottom of that pit, as the sun set on his hopes and dreams. Those dreams were dashed in the darkening fear of night, as uncertainty swept into every corner of his soul.

His body was covered with abrasions and cuts from the rocks and debris that had lacerated his tender skin. What was running through his mind? Would he ever see his father again? Through the tragedy of his mother's death, their relationship had become so close. How would they cope if they lost each other?

Perhaps his brothers would show repentance, he thought. Surely they would have a change of heart soon. They were still his brothers, after all…weren't they?

There was a thick smell of mold in the bottom of the moist, mud-caked well. As the chill of the pit slowly turned to warmth in the brilliant afternoon sun, hope was rekindled in Joseph's heart.

He heard the familiar voices of his brothers coming toward the pit, probably coming back to end this prank, he thought. Joseph's fear turned into peace. But what he did not realize was that slave merchants were also approaching; he had been sold for twenty pieces of silver.

Desperate, hungry, dirty, and bruised, Joseph was delivered up from the dismal pit into the hands of traders. With his hands tied tightly so he would not escape, he was taken away for the long journey to—who knew where? In shock and disbelief, he watched as his brothers laughed at him. He cried in terror for their mercy! Joseph had no idea where he was being taken. But this he did know: it would be far from the land of his birth and the father he greatly loved.

He could remember the times Jacob had held him securely, comforting his precious son. He could remember being raised by the beautiful Rachel, who waited many years for him. He was a son of promise, a gift from God! He had known the tenderness of loving, proud parents. But there he was, stripped of his dignity and being dragged behind a camel.

Stumbling in the intense heat of the unforgiving desert sun, Joseph's broken heart was filled with great sadness. What about the promise? What about the dreams? Joseph would ask these questions from the loneliest places of his heart and soul. *What has happened to my life? Could this really be happening to me?* They were like thoughts in slow motion during the seemingly endless seconds of time.

He was being thrust forward, completely at the bidding of the camel he was tied to. He didn't know whether he could survive the desert heat. It had been a glorious day, offering so much hope and promise, but it was ending with fear and uncertainty.

I imagine that it was a terrifying, sleepless night for Joseph. The wild thoughts about his safety and future were physically draining. His heart raced anxiously, pounding loudly in the chilly but silent desert night. Would this dark nightmare ever end? He endured moments of broken confusion as the shadows of the moon danced over the never-ending sand dunes of the unfamiliar desert. Along with the sounds of camels during the night, there would have been the occasional piercing, haunting howl of desert jackals as they sang into the dark atmosphere. The occasional hideous laughter of the greedy merchants, discussing the bargain they got at Dothan, added to his overwhelming sadness. My heart goes out to Joseph. He did not know what his future would hold. But he did know that it had been changed forever.

After many long miles of suffocating desert heat, Joseph arrived in Egypt, now a slave with lost hopes and forgotten dreams. He was unshaven and dirty from the desert dust that rolled off the camel's back. The strong, pungent smell of the beast was still heavy in the air, as were the flies that pestered Joseph. With his hands still in bondage, he could only shake his head to get rid of them.

What were Joseph's thoughts as he waited to enter the distant land of Egypt? Thoughts of home? Thoughts of his dearly missed mother and father? Would he ever see his father again? At this moment, it did not look like it.

He yearned for the land of his birth. It was the land promised to his great-grandfather Abraham—the "friend of God." Joseph must have wondered how the son of a promise could find himself in a foreign country. Where had the promise of God gone? What about Great-grandfather Abraham and his covenant with God? I am sure these thoughts, like wind-swept desert storms, raced through the weather-beaten, broken spirit of Joseph.

■ ■ ■

"The Lord saves the godly! He is their salvation and their refuge when trouble comes" (Ps. 37:39).

At times, we are much like Joseph when he was tied behind that camel; we are on an involuntary journey into the unknown.

When unexpected tragedies or the wrong choices of others test the very core of our being, we must keep our focus on the Lord and His promises for our life. If we don't, the journey we are on will become bleak, and the cry of our soul will be enormous.

We have choices to make when we find our lives at that fork in the road. We can choose to remain positive and make the unbearable situation better. Or we can fight our circumstances and make our life worse. In choosing the latter, we often take the misguided route of becoming bitter rather than better.

Why is this choice so dangerous? It is hard enough when events or tragedies strike the very nucleus of our souls. But when we choose to get resentful and bitter, we not only have the disaster to sort out but have also corrupted our future life with our sin. It is vital that we keep our thoughts fixed on the Lord.

■ ■ ■

" 'As for me, this is my promise to them,' says the Lord. 'My Holy Spirit shall not leave them, and they shall want the good and hate the wrong—they and their children and their children's children forever' " (Isa. 59:21).

Frightened at what might lie ahead, yet also knowing of God's promise on his young life, Joseph entered the empire of Pharaoh and the structured cities of Mitzriam, Egypt. He found himself tired and confused as he was led into his uncertain future in the strange yet interesting place.

As a boy, he had heard intriguing stories about Egypt. His father would tell how his great-grandma Sarah had met Pharaoh. Joseph would eagerly listen as his father told the "campfire stories" of the great things that God had planned for Abraham and his family. Joseph had thought he might like to visit Egypt sometime, just to see what Father Abraham had seen, but not under these circumstances. If Joseph could have been a shepherd in Egypt, at least he would have only been despised. But a slave? Joseph certainly knew that there was no way up for a slave.

"When Joseph arrived in Egypt as a captive of the Ishmaelite traders, he was purchased from them by Potiphar, a member of the personal staff of Pharaoh, the king of Egypt. Now this man Potiphar was the captain of the king's bodyguard and his chief executioner" (Gen. 39:1). We can only imagine what thoughts raced through Joseph's young mind as his hope evaporated into thin air, like faded memories of a forgotten promise. Where had God's promise disappeared to? But during this dark time in Joseph's life, God was shining a light on him which attracted the attention of Potiphar.

"The Lord greatly blessed Joseph there in the home of his master, so that everything he did succeeded. Potiphar noticed this and realized that the Lord was with Joseph in a very special way" (Gen. 39:2-3). The hand of God had set Joseph aside for greater purposes, so he was quickly elevated to a higher level of responsibility.

■ ■ ■

Whenever we find ourselves in an uncomfortable situation like Joseph's, it is important to remain calm and trust God. However, chaotic moments can make it difficult to do this, especially if our suffering is prolonged. Our nature is to wonder, *Why has this happened?*

I want to sincerely speak from my heart. There have been events in my life that made no sense to me. But the enemy's attempts to weaken my faith have actually, over time, given me greater endurance and insightful wisdom. So when things don't make any sense in your life, trust God. In time, He will restore what has been stolen from you, and the restoration will be astronomical in proportion to your suffering. Just don't give up!

God went ahead of Joseph, even during a period of disaster and confusion. If you find yourself in a similar situation, know that God has gone ahead of you and is preparing an avenue of safety for your protection. He is there with you! He has not abandoned you. He will give you favor with those around you. You will be brought to a level of safety during this crisis. I am here to encourage you, to let you know that your difficult situation will pass. The ability to overcome this injustice is already inside you. Be encouraged; God has gone ahead of you in this crisis, like he did with Joseph. Always pray for favor! It will be OK for you!

Because God showed favor on everything that Joseph did, Potiphar wanted to invest in him. It says that "Potiphar gave Joseph the complete administrative responsibility over everything he owned. He hadn't a worry in the world with Joseph there, except to decide what he wanted to eat!" (Gen. 39:6). There was a period of gracious favor given to Joseph.

God will also show you this favor. Trust Him! He will!

■ ■ ■

PRAYER OF ENCOURAGEMENT: Father, in Jesus' name I lift up my sisters and brothers in Christ. I impart into their life an anointing that will heal the injustice they may be going through. Father, I ask with a heartfelt compassion that you guard your people as they go through this period of transition. Lord, send angels of mercy, angels of protection, to cover your people in their time of struggle. Comfort your people, Lord, and help them recognize your abiding presence. You are with them and will never leave them or forsake them. Let the brilliant light of your glory shine into the "prisons" they find themselves in. Seal your people with the power of your Holy Spirit and send them warriors of mercy to deliver them into your arms where they can rest in safety. In Jesus' name, I release this anointing of comfort and compassion into their lives by the power of the blood of Jesus. No enemy can stand against your power that hovers over them. Bless your people, Father. Amen!

CHAPTER TWO

NINE/NINE/ EIGHTY-ONE

A Defining Moment that Tested My Character

We each have times or events in our lives that are special to our spirit. These precious moments of life are hidden tenderly in our hearts and cherished. One such thing in my life is autumn. I absolutely love that time of the year. With the winds of change, autumn ushers in a spirit of renewal. The crops are mature and the subtle warmth of an Indian summer approaches. When you look to the sky, you might see a flock of snow geese slowly fade into a brilliant orange, dusty-pink sunset. This special time of the year awakens my soul and means a lot to me. However, with the passing of time, that joy has diminished.

I remember clearly the autumn of 1981. I was nineteen. I was full of life and I had big dreams and great expectations for my future! The promises of hope for my future seemed so real and so attainable. I had graduated one year early from high school. During my junior and senior year, I was sixteen and working full-time to help provide for my family because my mother was a single parent, left with the insurmountable responsibility of raising five young and dynamic kids. (My father left when I was nine years old. A year later, my grandfather suddenly passed away, making me the oldest male in the family.) The family needed the support I could offer. So I became a pro at giving selflessly. I am so lucky that I had those experiences. They tried and tested me for leadership early. And later in life, they helped me to move mountains and accomplish great things for the Lord. When you have no agenda but the "good of all," you keep your focus on others. In this long process, you develop into a selfless leader who puts the safety of others first. As you walk with this humility, God will promote you.

■ ■ ■

Labor Day weekend had just passed, and I was looking forward to the autumn; not only did I love the harvest season but I also was an avid outdoor person and loved to hunt. I wasn't a very good hunter, but I loved being out in the woods in the early morning. There is so much activity as nature is animated by the rising of the sun. I treasure those memories; God was calling to my heart in a special way. It was in those moments that I often felt the presence of God and His promise of great plans for my life.

During times like that, you need to hang onto the promise of a better future. Your soul needs to recall those special moments when you are in a life-altering situation. In times of danger, we can cling to those, oven-warm, fresh bread-smelling memories. They give us hope and courage to survive just one more day.

I was getting ready to go to lunch and had planned on going to Waterloo, Iowa to pick up my entry in the KWWL TV-7 Labor Day Art Contest. I was already an accomplished artist and had plans for many great things. I had always wanted my art to win the Federal Duck Stamp Competition in Washington, D.C. I was always planning and looking to the future for the family that I was responsible for.

As I was heading out to lunch, I went into the office at the cooperative, and the secretary, Ardie, told me, "John, a semi just pulled in. Would you go and load him before your lunch break?" I was a responsible person, so I agreed. I went outside to the towering concrete elevator to prepare for the semi. He had come for a load of corn.

The elevator was about one hundred and forty feet tall and had concrete silos that stored over a hundred thousand bushels of grain. There were storage areas on each side of the driveway where the grain was either brought in for storage or loaded to be shipped out.

I entered the elevator to get the equipment ready to load the semi. I hadn't been in the elevator one minute when I heard an eerie, deafening, roaring, thundering sound from within the elevator shaft I was standing next to. As I turned around, a monstrous, glowing orange ball of fire engulfed me. I was in the center of a flash explosion!

Two minutes earlier, I had been heading off for lunch with my time card in hand; now I was at ground zero of a two thousand degree grain dust explosion. (I later learned that grain dust is ten times more explosive than dynamite!) The force of the blast threw me thirty feet, slamming me into a concrete silo. The explosion was so great that it was heard fourteen miles away and shook the entire town of La Porte City. Over a one-mile radius, people could actually feel the force of this sonic boom. It rattled windows in people's homes while it terrorized my life.

I thought to myself, *This is a dream. This can't be happening.* But the stark reality was that I was on fire and breathing in torrid flames. As the force of the explosion threw me, I landed face down in the corner of the elevator alleyway. I was very lucky to have landed face down. If I had landed face up, I might have lost my nose and lips to the intense heat of the explosion.

There was a heavy, three feet by six feet steel plate that covered the leg belt and buckets. The force of the explosion ripped it off, stripping the bolts. With rocketing force, the steel plate crushed the catwalk on the other side of the alleyway. As I was being catapulted into the air, I saw a heavy aluminum shovel fly past me. I watched in those micro-seconds—when time stood still and hell was magnified—as this shovel curled and melted under the intense heat. It looked like an open hand that was closing into a fist. I was totally conscious during all of this! As I lay there, still on fire, I thought again, *This can't be happening*. But, unfortunately, it was.

I used to love to get to work early, go to the top of the one hundred and forty foot elevator, and breathe in the pre-dawn moment. I would pray and watch the golden glow of the sun as it rose on the horizon, starting the new day. These moments were so special. I often think of the times I would get to work early and then sing to the Lord from inside the top of the elevator in the head house. But now, the place that had brought me joy was destroying me.

As I lay there, still on fire, this thought came to me: *I'll be ugly the rest of my life, and I won't be working out tonight.* It's funny what thoughts cross your mind during a crisis. It was Wednesday, and my brother Dave and I worked out every Monday, Wednesday and Friday. We had just made a large investment in a set of Olympic free weights. Even as all these thoughts sped through my mind, I felt that God gave me a choice: *Do you want to lay there and die? Or do you want to get up and live?*

I chose life! I got up and started to run. As I looked at my left arm, I saw my flesh hanging down from my fingertips in long strips. I remember thinking to myself, *I will not look at myself again.* I couldn't bear it. As the psalmist said, "Death stared me in the face—I was frightened and sad. Then I cried, 'Lord, save me!' ...I was facing death and then he saved me... I shall live! Yes, in his presence—here on earth!" (Ps. 116:3-9).

My younger brother David was also working at the cooperative. He was in the feed mill, bagging feed. After the blast, he came running and crying to me. I was still in flames. The only part of the shirt that wasn't on fire was a two-inch piece of my collar. David burned his hands as he put out the smoldering flames.

When the flames were extinguished, I ran to the office. I was yelling, "JESUS! HELP ME!" As I got to the office, a woman named Joy Shahan arrived. I later found out that Joy had been at her mother's home—two blocks away—when the force of the explosion lifted her out of her seat! She worked in the emergency unit of Schoitz Hospital in Waterloo, but it was her day off. She had always had a plan of action in case there was an explosion at the cooperative. I thank God she did. With burn patients, the first hour is critical, and her quick action saved my life. She told people to get the garden hose and spray me with water to cool me down. I told her, "No, I will crack!" I imagined the cool water splitting the skin on what was left of my body. At the same time, the semi driver, who had barely been spared from the flames, came to help. He had a jackknife, and they used it to cut my pants and boots off.

I was being prepared for the ambulance. In the aftermath of the explosion that rocked La Porte City, there was an eerie calm in the air. It was a day of abject silence. The thundering sonic boom that brought terror into my life also brought silence into their day. It seemed that even the birds quit singing on that beautiful September day.

Joy called the Schoitz emergency room and told them to be prepared for a critical burn trauma patient and to have the University of Iowa Hospital send their Air-Care helicopter. This timing was so important because my life was quickly fading away. The ambulance arrived, and Rick, my friend and co-worker, was on the ambulance team. He had been home for lunch when he heard the explosion.

Rick was also a firefighter. Amazingly, just five days before the accident, I had been with Rick when someone asked if he had ever seen a burn injury or death. Rick had been happy to reply that he hadn't. But all of that changed as Rick sat in quiet desperation next to me in the ambulance.

I told him, "Rick, don't leave me!" He didn't say very much to me because he was in shock. Jim, the ambulance driver, later told me, "Rick usually tells me to slow down when I am driving the ambulance. But that day he kept telling me to speed up." The trauma was also difficult for the paramedics and my brother Dave, who rode in the front of the ambulance on that unforgettable September day. It really ruined everyone's lunch.

I remember the overwhelming pain I was in as the ambulance sped to Waterloo. My legs still burned intensely. The rest of my body had third degree burns; even the nerve endings had been seared. So actually, the lighter, second-degree burns on my legs were most painful. In the ambulance, I just kept my eyes closed. But I remember the pain very vividly! I remember the searing heat that I felt on my legs. I kept asking the attendant to put more water on my legs. The pain was unbelievable. I found out later that it was Joy Shahan, and she recently told me, "John, when I ran out of water, it almost killed me when you kept asking for more water, because I didn't have any more." I recall the sound of them working near my ears; there was a crunching sound as Rick opened water containers. The intense heat of the explosion had burned the top off both my ears and had melted them to the side of my head. My hair was almost gone; it had melted, and there was also corn melted into the hair that was left.

It was a miracle that the ambulance arrived at Shoitz Hospital in about twelve minutes. The speeds averaged eighty miles an hour (the speed limit was fifty-five).

The staff hadn't believed Joy about the severity of the burns, but they had called the University of Iowa Hospital and had the Air-Care helicopter sent to Waterloo. The emergency room doctor, who had a Scottish accent, told me and his staff that my right arm would have to be amputated.

Now, *that* was not how I had planned to spend my lunch break.My first plan was full of enthusiasm, hope, and life as one who had a promising future as a wildlife artist. I was a youthful, optimistic and talented artist. (I won my first "Grand Champion and Peoples Choice Award" at a large regional art show when I was fifteen years old. And I started entering the Iowa duck, trout and habitat stamp competitions when I was sixteen.) I did not plan on being in the emergency room waiting for the University of Iowa Air-Care helicopter, hanging onto each and every second of my life!

At this time, my mother arrived. The other secretary, Marilyn, had driven to my home, picked up my mother, and brought her to me. I was amazed that she arrived so quickly, because we lived about thirty miles from Waterloo. I was glad to see her as they were getting me ready for the air transport. But what my mother saw would be a nightmare for any parent! Her oldest son was ravished with pain and the victim of critical burns. She told me, "John, you are going to be alright! I have called Stella Tosel, and we have people all around the world praying for you!"

And they did! This was a great comfort to me. I was so blessed to have that word of encouragement before I headed to the University Burn and Trauma Center. Stella is one of those real prayer warriors who won't take no for an answer. Neither did my mother—she was determined not to let her son die!

■ ■ ■

I was blessed to have a God-fearing mother who lived her faith. My mother was remarkable in that she never showed fear in the worst conditions in life. I guess it was something she learned from the hard things she had experienced.

My parents were missionaries in Papua New Guinea when they had just outlawed headhunting. She had many stories of events that challenged her and times she overcame life endangering situations. Mom and Senator Arthur Nue co-founded the Iowa Right to Life Committee. Because of her efforts, she received many death threats from lunatics. I honor her by saying that she had a resolute certainty about herself. The only way she survived raising five children alone was by walking in the power of the Holy Spirit. She walked in true obedience to God, true humility, and true love for God and people. These three things enabled her to come through to the other side. Now it was my time to learn these life lessons. I had been trained well by my mother, but it was up to God whether I would live to fulfill the purpose of my life.

I knew when I was twelve that God had a special purpose for me to fulfill as a very old man. I don't think the explosion was part of His plan. Jesus said, "The thief's purpose is to steal, kill and destroy. My purpose is to give life in all its fullness" (John 10:10).

■ ■ ■

I was conscious throughout all of this terrifying event. As I was rushed onto the helicopter, I joked with the nurse, saying, "How fast will this jet fly?" She must have thought I was delirious. I later found out that the motor they used in the helicopter actually was a jet motor.

I never cried or screamed out in pain. I remained very sensible and acutely tuned to every sound around me. I still had my eyes closed. The only time I opened them was when my mother came in or when the staff was examining me in the emergency room.

When there is a serious burn trauma, the medical staff is frantic, flying through their life-saving procedures. This is what happened when I arrived at the Burn Unit at the University of Iowa Hospital. Everything happened fast. I was in a very small room with all the staff around me. They had been notified of the explosion and were waiting for me. I was being prepared for the beginning of a horror story, the nightmare process that begins when you're on the journey out of a severe burn trauma. Words cannot adequately express the process that any severely burned patient must endure just to begin healing. These types of tragedies take time to recover from—not days or months but, unfortunately, years!

While I was in the unit, I was notified of what would happen to me in the next few hours. I was intubated because they knew my throat would swell shut. I was also told my eyes would swell shut for a number of days. I was being prepared for the never-ending measures of care I would receive during my stay in the Burn Unit. The intense process of stabilizing a burn patient is very detailed and finely tuned.

The television was on in the Burn Unit and they were talking about the explosion at the La Porte City Elevator where a nineteen-year-old man was critically burned. It is surreal to watch your life on television and, at the same time, experience the tragedy as it unfolds. The first time I thought of myself as a man was when they mentioned me on TV news.

As the doctors came in, they quietly talked among themselves about the condition of my burns. Even though they were talking in a hushed whisper, I heard all of the conversation. Doctor Albert Cram, Doctor Steven Jacobs, and the nursing staff were going through the charts to establish the severity and the percent of my body that was injured in the explosion. I heard them say, "He has burned over 68 percent of his body—second and third degree burns." This "news" that I wasn't supposed to hear did *not* comfort me.

I thank God for Joy Shahan's quick thinking to have Schoitz call for the AirCare and have the University get prepared. I was at the Burn Unit where I would get the best care. Whether I would live was another story. I was the most severely burned patient in the unit at the time. Would I die? Who knew at that time? The staff didn't know. My prognosis for survival was less than 20 percent.

But I knew that God had other plans for me. I praise God that He gave me a very godly mother who was bold and determined to not let her nineteen-year-old son die. She was a woman of incredible faith who always pressed through, even when a situation looked impossible. I was very blessed to be under her prayer covering and to hear confirmation from her earlier that day. It gave me the courage to hold on in the midst of a trauma I should not have survived.

I can not emphasize this point enough: encourage those around you. Yours may be the last word of encouragement they hear. They need a word of hope, inspiration or assurance to get them through a crisis, no matter how big. God had a plan for my life, and the enemy tried to take me out. It was crucial that I had a word from God about His plan for my life. We all need to know the plan God has specially chosen for us.

■ ■ ■

PRAYER OF ENCOURAGEMENT: Father, in Jesus' name, I pray from the very depth of my heart and soul that you give your people a vision of their purpose in life. Your people perish for a lack of vision. Father, equip your saints with the power of the Holy Spirit to be sincere encouragers of the brethren. Lord, give them power by the Holy Spirit to be servants of fire who move the obstacles in their world. Make them a determined people who stand in the gap for others. Let the light of your eternal Son, Jesus Christ the Messiah, shine from their very being. Let this light and love attract the wounded souls around them who are searching for their meaning in life. Father, I speak these words of life and faith over your people to equip them to be a blessing to those in desperate need. I seal it with the promise of the covenant of Jesus. And I release your power into their lives to be "vessels of encouragement" to those in need. Bless your people in the power of the blood of Jesus Christ!

CHAPTER THREE

GREATLY BRUISED, GREATLY USED

Maturity During Hardship

Whenever we find ourselves in difficult, life-threatening situations, we can choose to take what the enemy strategically planned to destroy us with and make it our friend. This is difficult, but extremely important for our survival! When we make the choice to do this, God steps in and gives us supernatural strength to be victorious by His might and glory! We then, being under the shadow of the Almighty, are given a place of rest for our soul, body, and spirit. In this great place of holy security, we are renewed daily. He imparts to us the knowledge we need to win the battles day by day. From this cocoon of protection, our inner soul can heal. God will turn around what the enemy meant to destroy our lives, and He will use us in those very areas to liberate and give freedom to captives. The Lord says, "You will live under a government that is just and fair. Your enemies will stay far away; you will live in peace. Terror will not come near" (Isa. 54:14).

In these very turbulent times, it is important to remain positive. That will be your greatest weapon and most effective tool in battling your situation. In these dangerous times, draw close to the Lord and you will find a great anointing as He surrounds you with an atmosphere of love and tender care. For you are created in His image, and He dearly loves you!

■ ■ ■

Young Joseph found his whole life turned upside down as he was taken where he didn't want to go. He made the long trek through the scorching noonday sun, with the sand blasting his face as the storms of the desert passed frequently by him. The ripe smell of camels and the stinging bite of sand fleas etched an imprint on his mind. But, sadly and with reserve, Joseph finally accepted where he was. As Joseph's tears slowly traveled down his dust-laden cheeks, he wondered, *Will I ever again see the land of my birth, the land of the promise?* He did not know, but with courage he faced the uncertainty.

In his darkest moments in Egypt, an inner strength quietly formed in Joseph. He faced the future knowing that his God was with him. During the brokenhearted moments of the frightened teenager's life, God was preparing the way for him. God's light would shine greatly on Joseph, and this illumination would gain him favor in a land of unknown cultures and strange people. So a period of gracious favor was given to Joseph. For twelve months, he managed and coordinated all the business affairs of Potiphar's household.

But then there was trouble. Potiphar's wife became interested in the handsome Joseph. After repeatedly failing to seduce him, she falsely accused Joseph of trying to assault her. This infuriated Potiphar, and he had Joseph thrown into prison.

There must have been a familiar ringing in his ears as the gates of the prison slammed shut, reminding him of the freedom he lost when he was sold into slavery. I am sure his heart sank as his chances for success were destroyed by the lust and lies of another. As Proverbs 13:12 says, "Hope deferred makes the heart sick." I'm sure Joseph was heartsick when he once again found himself in a hollow, empty pit.

We repeatedly find Joseph in the process of being broken. Yet God was molding a young boy into a visionary man who would save his own people as well as the entire empire of Egypt. But from his chains and shackles, Joseph longed simply for his home and the people he loved. Was his Father OK? Had his broken heart healed? These questions echoed in young Joseph, bound in chains as he watched the rats scurry by.

Shackled, shattered, and disillusioned, Joseph found himself again in a prison not of his making. This dark climate was intensified as a sinister cockroach crawled up his leg. The air was thick with the aroma of fellow prisoners and moldy straw. The sound of the heavy chains moving and degenerate prisoners bitterly complaining must have added to the darkness of Joseph's world. And this experience was made more painful by the injustice of being there for something he didn't do. His prayers might have been like these cries of David:

> Please, Lord, rescue me! Quick! Come and help me! Confuse them! Turn them around and send them sprawling—all these who are trying to destroy me. Disgrace these scoffers with their utter failure! But may the joy of the Lord be given to everyone who loves him and his salvation. May they constantly exclaim, "How great is God!" I am poor and needy, yet the Lord is thinking about me right now! O my God, you are my helper. You are my Savior; come quickly, and save me. Please don't delay! (Ps. 40:13-17).

What brought Joseph through this great series of injustices was the knowledge that God had not abandoned or forgotten him. Even in this turmoil, his faith was strong.

But the Lord was with Joseph there, too, and was kind to him by granting him favor with the chief jailer. In fact, the jailer soon handed over the entire prison administration to Joseph, so that all the other prisoners were responsible to him (Gen. 39:21-22).

Even when Joseph was in prison, God gave him favor. I often wonder about the growth process Joseph endured as his life slowly ebbed away. He was eighteen years old when he entered prison and thirty when he was released. This means Joseph spent twelve birthdays in prison! There was no family around, not many who really cared. From the darkness of his prison cell, how did Joseph carry on with the knowledge that he might never see light again? He held onto the promise that God had given first to his great-grandfather, Abraham:

> Leave your own country behind you, and your own people, and go to the land that I will guide you to. I will bless you and make your name famous, and will make you a blessing to many others. I will bless those who bless you and curse those who curse you; and the entire world will be blessed because of you (Gen. 12:1-3).

This promise was something his father Jacob talked about frequently. This "word of knowledge" that was passed down to Joseph gave him hope, insight, and the courage to withstand the pain of the terrifying loneliness he faced each and every day. It was this "hope of the promise" that gave Joseph the strength and endurance to continue. One thing that helped Joseph was that he found favor with the chief jailer; this gave him the ability to rise in the prison ranks. It also offered some relief from the mundane prison life, which slowly dripped on, one second at a time, one moment at a time, one day at a time.

■ ■ ■

Like Joseph, we all have had times in our lives when justice simply disappeared. When these "gasping for breath" moments happen, we need to take inventory of our life and realize that the way we handle ourselves in the face of injustice will often influence the outcome. If we choose to maintain our integrity, God will restore us by lifting us to a place of honor. Joseph could not understand in his mind what was happening, but his *heart* knew that God would make things right in time. The key is to stay focused on God's special promise for your life during adversity. Remember what God did for Joseph. He will do the same in your life!

In his broken and bruised state in prison, Joseph became a man. His character developed into the type of man God could use greatly. Often God's greatest plan to deliver you is in motion when it seems like there is little or no hope at all. In those empty, dark moments of life that we all face, God will elevate you. His glory will be greater than the circumstances you find yourself in. Joseph experienced this, having become a broken, yielded vessel. From his experience emerged a story of greatness. God did this by pouring His power and strength into a weak vessel, for the glory of His kingdom. While in prison, Joseph's feet were crippled by shackles, but his *spirit* matured, empowering him to become a humble visionary.

I imagine that the long, desolate nights brought remembrance of the "gift" God had given him many years before. Or perhaps he forgot some of the dreams because of the hardships. He entered Egypt as a terrified teenager, but developed into a visionary giant who would rescue his people, save Egypt, and become close friends with Pharaoh. It is amazing how God worked everything out! It is so important to continue trusting God, even when things look hopeless.

> Some time later it so happened that the king of Egypt became angry with his chief baker and his wine taster, so he jailed them both in prison where Joseph was, in the castle of Potiphar, the captain of the guard, who was the chief executioner. They remained under arrest there for quite some time, and Potiphar assigned Joseph to wait on them (Gen. 40:1-4).

During those moments, Joseph had a glimpse of hope. Then came his time for redemption and honor. When a great injustice has been dealt to you, God will also honor you greatly. Just hang in there until the fulfillment of the promise. You will soon be saying, "The Lord rewarded me for doing right and being pure" (Ps. 18:20).

The hard lessons and training of prison made Joseph into a remarkable man, one who stood head and shoulders above the rest—and he passed the test. Instead of becoming bitter from the injustice he had gone through, he chose to make the best of each situation. In a darkened prison cell, God was molding him into a vessel that would do mighty things for His glory.

The unpredictable clouds in Joseph's life lifted, and God's favor and glory were evident on the young man as he was being prepared to meet Pharaoh. Pharaoh had received two disturbing dreams, and none of the court magicians could interpret them. The cup-bearer, remembering Joseph and his interpretations, told the Pharaoh, and "Pharaoh sent at once for Joseph. He was brought hastily from the dungeon, and after a quick shave and change of clothes, came in before Pharaoh" (Gen. 41:14).

God had prepared Joseph for the greater work of saving the Hebrews. It was an important statement of faith that in front of Pharaoh Joseph gave all the glory to God. " 'I can't do it by myself,' Joseph replied, 'but God will tell you what it means!' " (Gen. 41:16). When you have this attitude of humility, God will greatly promote you. This is how Joseph went from prisoner to governor of Egypt, all in a matter of hours.

After Joseph correctly interpreted the dreams, God directed the thoughts of the righteous king.

Turning to Joseph, Pharaoh said to him, "Since God has revealed the meaning of the dreams to you, you are the wisest man in the country! I am hereby appointing you to be in charge of this entire project. What you say goes, throughout all the land of Egypt. I alone will outrank you" (Gen. 41:39-40).

What a restoration in such a short time! The Lord had given Joseph much favor in the eyes of the Pharaoh. He then made Joseph in charge of the entire land of Egypt. He placed a signet ring on his finger and put a gold chain around his neck. The Pharaoh dressed him in the finest clothes. Joseph's years of imprisonment were over, and the joy of being restored was complete.

That very average morning of Joseph's life started in the dungeon. But by evening, he was ruler of Egypt, finely dressed, and having supper with his new "best friend," the Pharaoh, the most powerful man in the world. Joseph's faithfulness in the small things paid off in the panorama of his life, much more than he could have ever imagined when he was just a terrified teenager being ripped from his home and sold into slavery.

God is truly faithful in all of His plans, and He promises that He will never abandon you in your time of darkness. He says, "No, I will not abandon you or leave you as orphans in the storm—I will come to you" (John 14:18).

What a precious promise we have from our Redeemer. Remember the Word of God in your time of trouble. With time and faithfulness, you will be restored to a greater position than you had before. What the enemy meant for evil, God will use for the glory of His kingdom, and you will also be honored in the process. God sees your faithfulness, and He will greatly reward you for your sacrifice. He truly loves you! Yes—as Joseph was restored, you shall be too. I encourage you in this!

God restored Joseph's life just as suddenly and quickly as it had been taken from him. And this time, Joseph was more mature, humble, and willing to do God's will. The process of being broken is often extremely painful. But the results are a restored life operating in victory that is to be greatly admired! After having his hopes, dreams, and life greatly bruised, Joseph found himself empowered to be greatly used. This plan of redemption was God-ordained because it not only saved the empire of Egypt but also saved his own family and the inherited promise of Abraham. God is so good! "The Lord is my light and my salvation; whom shall I fear?" (Ps. 27:1).

■ ■ ■

PRAYER OF ENCOURAGEMENT: Father, in Jesus' name, I ask that you send people to encourage those who are hurting and going through a difficult time. Send them messengers of light, just at the right time when they need to hear a word from you, Father. Cover your people with a great anointing of comfort. Let it be like a blanket of love that covers them from head to toe. Father, in this covering of light and love, reassure your saints that they, too, will be restored to a greater level than they can imagine today! I ask that the Holy Spirit will witness and confirm this today. Let this day be the beginning of a new life restored in Christ. Each morning, Father, let there be new mercies and melodies from the Holy Spirit to encourage and comfort your people! I seal this in the person of the Holy Spirit by the power of the atoning blood of Jesus! I ask it, Father! Amen.

CHAPTER FOUR

COURAGE
UNDER FIRE

I Shall Not Die,
but Live to Tell of All His Deeds!

This certainly was not the perfect ending to an incredibly beautiful day. My morning had started with hope and great expectations. But, unfortunately, I was now in the University of Iowa Hospital Burn Unit with critical burns. The probability of survival was in God's hands and in my determination not to give up. My only advantage was my youth; an older person may not have survived. A burn victim's body is so compromised by the trauma that every organ works overtime to establish a sense of normalcy. You cannot imagine what this very long process is like.

In the Burn Unit, the doctors and nursing staff feverishly tried to stabilize my condition. I thank God for the nursing staff, Dr. Cram, and Dr. Jacobs. They closely monitored my condition. The first thing they did was intubate me. That is tough, especially when you are awake. You have to swallow the tube that keeps your esophagus clear. My esophagus would have swollen shut otherwise. I remember my throat burning as the tube was inserted.

Then, there were many other procedures to follow. Whenever there is a critical burn, intensive care is required, such as antibacterial dressings to cover the wounds. The patient often becomes dehydrated and is in danger of going into shock. Intravenous solutions are necessary to provide fluids and nutrients. A nasogastric tube is passed from the nose into the stomach to prevent vomiting. The contents of the stomach are then suctioned. A Foley catheter is then placed to drain the bladder. The patient's heart rhythm is closely monitored. Breathing may become difficult, and the patient may require assistance in the form of oxygen and humidity. With severe burns such as mine, it was necessary to have all of these treatments to prevent shock and other complications. I was beginning the roller coaster ride of a lifetime.

■ ■ ■

I want to take this time to encourage those of you who are going through a difficult time. The most important point I can make is this: don't look too closely at the details of the situation. Trust that God will bring you through your trial. He will provide supernatural strength to help you endure. In the midst of trials, the enemy often comes like a thief to try to steal your faith. David said, "On the day when I was weakest, they attacked. But the Lord held me steady. He led me to a place of safety, for he delights in me" (Ps. 18:18-19).

If you are in a difficult situation, take the time to restore and strengthen your faith by getting into God's Word. God has a very special plan for you. Set your sights on His faithfulness. Keep your focus on Jesus. During the trial, He may be all you have the energy for, but He won't disappoint you.

It is so important to keep your faith life in good condition before a disaster, rather than trying to locate it the midst of the trial. Know that God only wants good for you, and you must keep in mind that He really does love you.

■ ■ ■

I remember feeling exhausted as my body worked overtime to repair itself. The thick gauze dressings covering my wounds were soaked in silver nitrate, an antibacterial agent. Even the walls wore a thick splattering of this black substance that left permanent stains on everything it touched.

As difficult as these events were, I was painfully aware that it was only the beginning of the journey to my recovery. A burn victim's body undergoes many changes as the bodily defense systems rush to the wounded tissues.

■ ■ ■

At one point my heart stopped. I had a cardiac arrest, and I actually died.

It was early in the morning, about 2 a.m., the same night I arrived at the burn unit. Suddenly, my body went into violent convulsions. Cardiac arrests are different than heart attacks. In a cardiac arrest, your heart stops. I remember seeing the doctors and nurses frantic as I went into convulsions and a code blue. I screamed in my spirit to my mother to pray for me (I later heard that she was jolted out of bed at the very time of my trouble). Then I entered an incredibly peaceful darkness. I had such a feeling of peace, wholeness and love in the hands of God. It gave me comfort that God was in control, as I had no energy to help myself. This experience was incredibly peaceful, a pleasant rest from the trauma. As I rested in that peaceful darkness, I heard the Lord telling me, *Don't fight this! Lay under it and you will be OK!* And that is what I did. I did not have the physical energy to help myself.

Recently a Christian motivational speaker was on Dr. James Dobson's radio program, "Focus on the Family," and she told of her after-death experience. She also had a cardiac arrest. Our experiences were exactly the same, so I listened carefully. She described it as a warm womb of God's love.

■ ■ ■

In those very dark moments of our lives, we often feel helpless, and I certainly did. But in those moments, God's power manifests most greatly and shines most brilliantly. You don't have to survive an explosion to experience this. Life frequently presents us with circumstances we can't control. When we are weak, God's great mercy and grace are there to see us through. Remember that the Bible says, "Wait for the Lord, and he will come and save you! Be brave, stouthearted and courageous. Yes, wait and he will help you" (Ps. 27:14).

It was at this crossroads that I found myself. I was very fortunate that Dr. Steven Jacobs was on duty that night. It was through his efforts that my lifeless body was revived at 2 a.m. I knew it was not the appointed time for me to die. It had been impressed upon me at the age of twelve that God had a very special assignment involving Israel for me to fulfill. I was confident that I would live to be a very old man so that I could fulfill that promise. I often motivated myself to endure the pain and difficulties with this confidence. I was determined to fulfill that word.

When I saw the photos of how I looked upon my arrival at the Burn Unit, I was astounded. It appeared as though I had emerged from an incinerator. Years later, it's hard to resurrect all of the difficult memories, but I remember enough to realize how far God has brought me. I'm truly an amazing testimony of survival. It is very difficult to see your progress when you're in the midst of a trial. But with the gift of time, you will look back in awe at God's mercy in bringing you through with a renewed sense of purpose.

Recently, this became real to me while I was in Kiev, Ukraine. I had been following the progress of a young South African man who burned 80 percent of his body in a house fire in America. I had been encouraging his wife and family, and the day I left for America, I received the news that he did not survive. My heart was so sad. It made me understand that my survival was a miracle and that God has a story for me to tell.

Following the death experience, I was moved to the unit where I would receive more one-on-one care. My condition was critical. There was a male orderly who said, "You had a very rough night." Since my arrival in the unit I hadn't been allowed any food or water. The orderly was a very kind and gentle individual, and he mercifully gave me some ice to quench my relentless thirst. Imagine being so incapacitated that you must depend on others for your very basic needs. Maybe you are in a situation like that too. During situations like this, you must trust God and completely surrender to Him. If you do, those dark, hellish moments will prove to be the most empowering times of your life. God will fully take over. Suddenly, the hopeless despair will turn into a brilliant display of God's love!

■ ■ ■

My survival was moment by moment. I was not expected to live. As my eyes swelled shut and I lived in literal darkness for several days, I tried to understand what had happened to my life that had once held so much hope. I drifted in and out of consciousness, trying to gauge my progress by listening to the comments of the staff.

This reminds me of times in Israel's history when her life was nearly cut off. Every time, God mercifully saved Israel for His glory! The word *Holocaust*, which in Hebrew means "a sacrifice consumed by fire," was one of mankind's darkest events. However, this tiny nation has arisen stronger and more unified as a result. The same principle applies to our difficult circumstances.

One thing you will never forget if you are a patient in a Burn Unit (or if you're brave enough to visit one), is the smell of burned flesh and hair. The odor of chlorine, used to sanitize the whirlpool baths, also permeates the humid air.

I was aware that I had many surgical procedures ahead of me. Once I was out of Intensive Care and back in the Burn Unit, I was able to reflect on the multitude of cards and well-wishes I had received. I was very well liked and had always tried to be good to people. At work, I made an intentional effort to remember people's names. I would find out things about individuals so that I could more effectively converse with them and be sincere.

Those first days in the Burn Unit were so long, and I was incredibly sick and weak. As I drifted in and out of consciousness, I was aware of my family visiting. It was a very difficult time for my mother; she didn't want to lose her firstborn son. She stood her ground with the staff and made sure I received the best treatment.

The first operation following my accident was to debride the damaged skin. Debridement is a process of shaving away all the skin that has died as the result of the burns. Sheets of fresh pigskin called "xenografts" are applied over the debrided areas and fresh dressings are applied. For most burn victims, this process is repeated approximately every five days. When possible, sheets of the patient's own skin called "autografts" are applied. The donor sites for this skin are actually as painful as the burned areas.

One session of debridement was to remove pieces of grain that had been embedded in my skin. In addition, the clothing I had been wearing had melted into my skin. Had I been wearing the khaki pants that matched my shirt, I would have sustained third degree burns on over 97 percent of my body. God spared me the worst. I had worn blue jeans that day, and even though they were in flames, they did not complicate the injuries by melting to my flesh. As a result, the burns on my ankles and legs were only second degree.

Once I awoke from surgery, I realized that I had no use of my right arm—absolutely none. The pain was unbelievable. There had been discussion of amputating the arm, but my mother was determined to stand in the way of that. I recall telling her that something had gone wrong in surgery. The surgeons had to go deep into the soft tissues during the debridement process and there was some damage to the nerves as a result. My arm was in a lot of pain, and I couldn't move it at all. It was as if it had gone to sleep, yet the pain was incredible. Sometimes it made it difficult to breathe, even years after the accident.

To my horror, I also lost the use of my left arm for a time, but it miraculously recovered from the numbness. I was greatly relieved! However, with all of the bandages on, I couldn't even feed myself. I needed help for the simplest of tasks, like drinking water.

I lay in bed with my arms outstretched. My arms were supported by wing-like attachments on either side of the bed. My head had swollen to the size of a pumpkin, and I was wrapped in bandages from head to toe. Some of the visitors who came to see me stayed only briefly and didn't return. But several friends came to see me regularly. One was Patti Paca, a student at the University of Iowa studying ophthalmology. Rob Legge, a friend from high school, was an occasional visitor who later told me he had recognized me only by my nose, the one area not concealed by bandages.

Several more sessions of debridement were undergone to remove dead tissue and limit the possibility of infection. Daily debridement sessions in the whirlpool tank became routine, and the strong smell of chlorine became commonplace. A bleach solution was added to the water in the whirlpool tank to inhibit bacterial growth. The process of debridement while in the whirlpool bath was incredibly painful; a spoon-like instrument was used to scrape the dead tissue away. Another patient in the unit was in horrendous pain, and her loud, piercing screams terrified the rest of the patients. I had determined that when it was my turn, I would "bite the bullet" and not vocalize my pain. However, my silence concerned the staff and they actually told me, "John, it's OK to scream." I responded that I would not because it wouldn't make their job any easier.

Following the torturous sessions of debridement, Silvadene Cream was applied to thick strips of bandages and the wounds were bandaged once again. This process of re-bandaging was slow and painstaking and took a lot of bandages. I'm a large man, so it was a tall order. My energy was completely sapped by this daily process.

Human skin, the body's largest organ, provides the function of normalizing the temperature. Burns as extensive as mine result in heat loss. Artificial heat is provided with radiant lamps, warm rooms, and blankets. One night I shivered so violently that my teeth chattered. The nurse kept coming in to add blankets, and by the end of the night, I had accumulated seventeen of them! It was nearly impossible to move under the weight, but at last I was warm! God bless her; she was so kind to me.

When I had the debridement surgeries, the pigskin grafts were applied until I had adequate donor sites to supply the autografts. There was hardly enough viable skin with which to take an adequate graft. To this day the graft areas on my legs are visible. I'm scarred from the top of my head to my ankles, but the scars have faded so you would hardly know it. I can still see small strips near my ankles where grafts were taken for my fingers.

Joy Shahan, the paramedic who was one of the first on the scene of my accident, recently told me that they were unsure I would survive. She had thought I would at least lose all of my fingers. Praise God that did not happen, especially since I am an author and creative person.

King David reminds us, "Weeping may go on all night, but in the morning there is joy" (Ps. 30:5). I wonder if the psalmist, through the Holy Spirit, was talking about Joy Shahan? Through her, I have learned to see humor and be able to express it in my life. Since I do not easily forget people who have helped me, I recently wanted to do something special for Joy. So I asked her what dream she may have held onto since childhood. She said: "Even my husband and children don't know this. I have always wanted to play the harp." So I hired a duet team to do a violin-harp recital in her home. It was very special for Joy. She said the recital gave the home a special feeling of peace.

My Irish humor has given me the eternal eyes to see me through many hard trials. That is a gift I learned from my mother. She had such a hard life and did many selfless things for others, yet she always managed to laugh at the end of the day. It was a very good example for me to follow. I was in a situation where I certainly needed it, so I had an opportunity to practice this lifesaving lesson.

My longest surgery was nine hours, performed by Dr. Steven Jacobs. This procedure focused on removing clothing that had melted to my skin and preparing the donor sites.

Following the procedures to graft skin onto my hands, I was introduced to a hideous device that would help my hands and fingers heal. This contraption was constructed of a twelve-inch, wooden embroidery hoop with eyelets strategically attached. Cloth mesh tube-type bandages were attached to my fingers, protecting the autografts. Small metal hooks were glued to my fingernails, and then thick rubber bands were stretched from the hooks to the hoop. This created traction for my fingers so they would not contract during the healing process. It was painless but extremely awkward, as you can imagine. I was totally immobile and completely helpless to do anything for myself with these paddle-like devices attached to my hands. The Burn Unit must have looked like a chamber of horrors to visitors.

Visitors dwindled as time passed. My health was suddenly declining and it seemed I wasn't progressing. I continued to move in and out of consciousness, and sleep brought delirious nightmares instead of rest. I would cry out for help as I relived that day at the cooperative. I would be loading a semitruck up on the catwalk, but I had so many bandages on my hands that I couldn't close the chute as the grain poured from the overhead bin. The corn was about to overflow the top of the semi. As you'll recall, that is what I was doing at the moment of the explosion. In the dream, the Burn Unit nurse would be taking me back to my room and I would be yelling that I had to shut off the flow of the grain. When I was dreaming, I would shout out orders, as I did in my job as foreman, directing my employees to get their work done. Even in my recuperation, I was taking responsibility for getting the job done! Inevitably, the dreams concluded with nurses coming to the cooperative to return me to the Burn Unit.

During this period of time, I was not getting better. I have some memories but not many. I do recall a fellow burn patient named Andrew, a Mennonite. Late one evening I heard strange singing. I honestly thought I had died and was in heaven. I couldn't understand the words to this music. It was nearing the end of visiting hours and Andrew had a number of German-speaking Mennonites visiting. They were singing in German. That was a jolt because I thought I was dead! Those days were particularly hard for me and my family. I had been in the Trauma Unit for over a month, and I didn't seem to be healing.

During this time, another medical professional had been added to my case. Tracy was a very attractive physical therapist. To me, she resembled the actress Morgan Fairchild. Physical therapists have to be very insistent with their patients in order to motivate them to push past their reluctance and pain.

Tracy reminded me of an angel. That's how I chose to view her visits on Monday mornings. She was a break from my dismal, gray existence. Her visits gave me hope, and she was an encouragement to me. Part of Tracy's routine was to ask me questions to assess my orientation to time and place. She would say, "Where are you, John?" Sometimes I would answer, "Mercy Hospital," and sometimes I would say, "Iowa City."

The Medical Staff were becoming concerned that I wasn't progressing. My stay in the Burn Unit for nearly five weeks had not brought the results they hoped for. They were concerned that I could have blood poisoning from the grain dust and material that they had removed from my burned flesh. The doctors stood in my room as they discussed the situation, poring over my medical record to determine what needed to be done. I was extremely groggy, but I remember hearing, "Now, you're not going to feel a thing."

One of the nurses held my leg while the doctor took a scalpel and cut a gash in my ankle. This was the site where they would begin blood transfusions. They repeated the process on the other leg, and I thought to myself, *Damn, I felt everything!*

Their diagnosis was correct. I had become toxic from the foreign materials embedded in my skin. I had been slowly dying, and the staff discovered it just in time!

■ ■ ■

In a matter of days following that close call, I was being assisted by a staff member in a walk down the hall. (One focus of physical therapy is to get the patient up and moving as soon as possible.) As we walked by Tracy, I heard her make an uncharacteristic mistake, stating that the University of Iowa was Mercy Hospital. My response amazed the staff. I said, "Tracy, what hospital are you in?" This was amazing, due to the fact that brain damage was a very real possibility. Now I was asking Tracy the question she had always asked me. The doctor on duty began to laugh in amazement because he knew my comment meant I was aware and oriented. Everyone was very pleased.

This incident was a turning point in my recovery, and the staff on the Burn Unit became confident that I would recover. Prior to that point, it hadn't looked very promising. Frequently, burn patients die from pneumonia or infection. This is why every burn unit is extremely cautious about cleanliness and asking visitors to gown and mask. The patients are extremely vulnerable.

During the time when I was so ill from blood poisoning, I barely remember my visitors. A former co-worker named Bob Christy visited with a friend, Ron Elwick, who was a City Councilman in Vinton at that time. Bob was in tears as he came in asking, "How's my boy?" My mother told me of their visit when I was aware. In later visits with Bob, he told me I had looked "like a skinned rabbit."

I wasn't completely out of the woods yet and continued to undergo treatment for my wounds. The donor sites were covered with iodine bandages to aid in healing. When doing research for this book, I looked at my medical history for the first time in twenty-one years. I found the photos taken at the hospital. The donor sites were as vividly red as the burned areas. I've included only select photographs to share in this book to prevent disturbing anyone with the graphic nature of the trauma I endured. I have had contact with the first paramedics on the scene following my accident, and it seems likely that my injuries were the worst they had ever seen up to that time. My hope is that they will not have to endure worse.

■ ■ ■

He gives power to the tired and worn out, and strength to the weak. Even the youths shall be exhausted, and the young men will all give up. But they that wait upon the Lord shall renew their strength. They will mount up with wings like eagles; they shall run and not be weary; they shall walk and not faint (Isa. 40:29-31).

Following the incident with Tracy and the other medical staff, it surprised everyone how quickly I rebounded. They could not believe it, calling me a miracle! I had not responded to treatment in the five weeks I was at the unit, and now I was rapidly recovering. God really does give power to the weak. I was living proof. It seemed the following days went quickly with the routine of daily physical therapy and treatment for wound recovery.

Aside from the effects of my injuries, my appearance had greatly changed. At the time of the accident, I had been regularly working out and was in great shape. At six feet two inches, I had weighed one hundred and ninety-five pounds. But I had dropped at least fifty-five pounds of muscle. I must have looked pretty pathetic. However, my eyes glistened with life and zeal to finish the race I was on, by the grace of God. I had to increase my caloric intake to twelve thousand just to hold my weight and begin to recover healthy tissue and muscle mass. I endured lots of protein shakes. Even though they tasted very bad, I knew they were important to my health and recovery.

The Burn Unit staff began to discover my personality. Up to this point, I had been little more than an unresponsive, badly burned body. Now I was *active* and full of *life!* I began to have fun with the staff. The visitors had trailed off, but I still had my daily routine.

The doctors could not determine why I had lost the use of my right arm. I carried it with either my left hand or a sling— it was so painful! The conclusion they finally reached was a diagnosis called, "idiopathic synthesis." In layman's terms, this means symptoms of unknown origin—they didn't know. I was evaluated by the Neurological Department. There I met a very kind Japanese doctor who explained that the cause of the dysfunction was undetermined but the nerve endings were intact. He said I would regain use of my arm but that it would be a slow, painstaking process over a period of years. He predicted that my arm would gain in strength about a millimeter per day. I was comforted by this evaluation and by the advice I was given to regain function in my arm and hand. I had been depending on my left hand and was continually challenged by something as simple as using a spoon left-handed. Even my left hand was compromised to about 50 percent of normal function.

One step necessary for my discharge from the Burn Unit was the fitting of the pressure suit. This suit is constructed of a thick, tan elastic material and, to be effective, must be much smaller than the individual. The purpose of this garment is to maintain pressure on the burned areas in order to flatten the scarred tissue. This is obviously uncomfortable and, honestly, makes the wearer look horrifying. Wearing the suit is somewhat of a nightmare, but its purpose is worth the discomfort. I wore the body suit and gloves for almost four years. I also had one for my face. As awkward as they look, they actually provide a sense of security, and they do their job of minimizing scar tissue thickness.

■ ■ ■

It was close to Halloween, and I was feeling up to pulling a prank with another patient named Joanne. She was unable to walk and was in a wheelchair. We "escaped" the Burn Unit one evening and went to the hospital lobby. In the lobby, it was obvious that someone had taken great care to prepare a decorative display for Halloween. Joanne and I stole a few small pumpkins and gourds from the display. Since I could use only one arm, I rested my hand on the wheelchair while she propelled herself with the wheels. Once back in "lock-up" on the Burn Unit, we shared with some of the staff what we'd done. We were the least likely of the unit's patients to pull such a prank, but it gave us such a sense of fun and adventure. The staff just laughed at us. Thinking back on that evening, I imagine how I looked—no hair and sickly looking with a fiery-red complexion, blue eyes, and a huge smile!

One day while I was in the Physical Therapy Department, I

mentioned to Tracy that I felt I had so much living to do. I had such a sense of disappointment. The weekends were long and lonely with hardly any visitors. I didn't know how much longer I could endure this pattern of life. Tracy said that I would probably be released the following week, according to my progress.

■ ■ ■

At last, the day came when Dr. Cram released me for the following day—October 30, 1981. I had become somewhat of a hero on the Burn Unit because of my fight to live and the amazing hand of God on my life. My mother's prayers had been answered. My courage, along with the excellent care provided by the staff, allowed me to overcome incredible odds. I hadn't been expected to live, let alone be released from the Burn Unit in less than ninety days. However, fifty-one days after the explosion, I was alive and heading home. What a miracle!

> I bless the holy name of God with all my heart. Yes, I will bless the Lord and not forget the glorious things he does for me. He forgives all my sins. He heals me. He ransoms me from hell. He surrounds me with lovingkindness and tender mercies. He fills my life with good things! My youth is renewed like the eagle's! (Ps. 103:1-5).

Some photos I found recently were taken at the time of my discharge from the Burn Unit. My mother was there to take me home. As I was having my photos taken, I began to cry uncontrollably. Up to that point, I had not cried. The nurse said she had never seen anyone cry so hard. I think I was aware that the journey was not going to get easier, but harder.

■ ■ ■

PRAYER OF ENCOURAGEMENT: Father, in Jesus' name I ask that you help those who are in a transition. They are moving from one difficult situation into another even more trying experience. Lord Jesus, give them the power and courage to be victorious where they are. Help them, Holy Spirit. Resurrect their lives with the same resurrection power that raised Jesus from the grave. Holy Spirit, I ask that you empower your people with the gift of comfort. Be with them in this time of need. Become so real to them that your glory is evident in the midst of tragedy! In Jesus' name, I speak protection and ask that warring angels surround your people, keeping them safe in this transition!

Photo courtesy of the Globe Gazette

Above: Having won the State of Iowa sharp shooting competition, I was heading for regionals. At the age of twelve, I had a determined focus and belief in God's promise and plan for my life. *Left:* At the age of fourteen, I was overflowing with hope (and wearing my favorite "shirt of many colors").

Above: At age fifteen I entered a large regional art show and won first place, Grand Champion and the Peoples Choice Award. *Right:* With "Uncle Rags" a few days before the explosion.

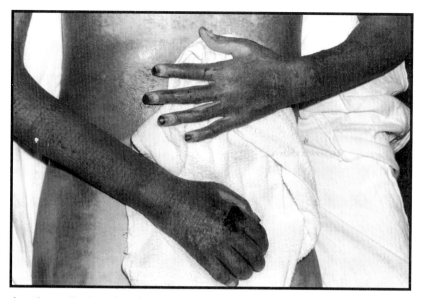

Are these the hands of an artist? That was the last thing on my mind; I was just trying to survive.

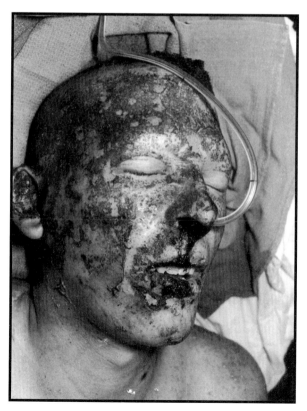

This is how I looked upon my arrival at the University of Iowa Burn Unit.

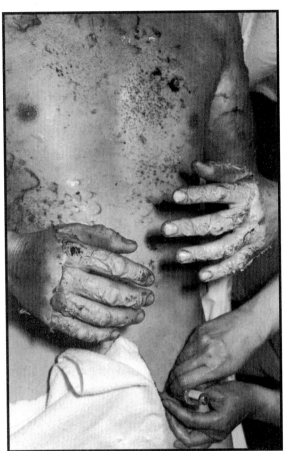

Left: Being brave while receiving a morphine shot to help with the extreme pain. *Below:* Weak and fragile, I was about to be dismissed from the unit. The donor sites on my legs where the grafts were taken were as painful as the burns.

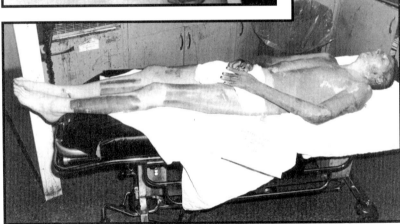

Photos courtesy of the University of Iowa Hospital

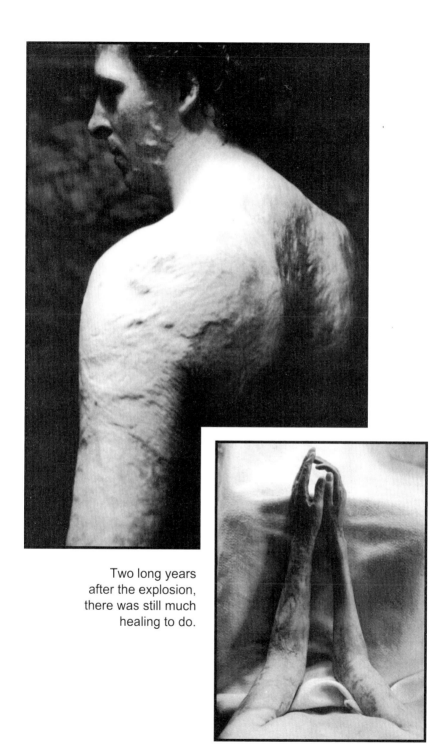

Two long years
after the explosion,
there was still much
healing to do.

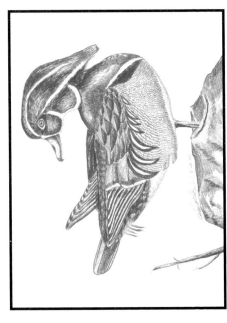

Wood duck pencil drawing.

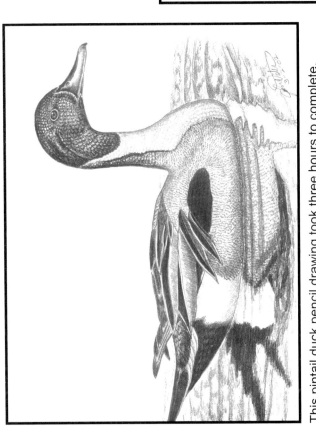

This pintail duck pencil drawing took three hours to complete.

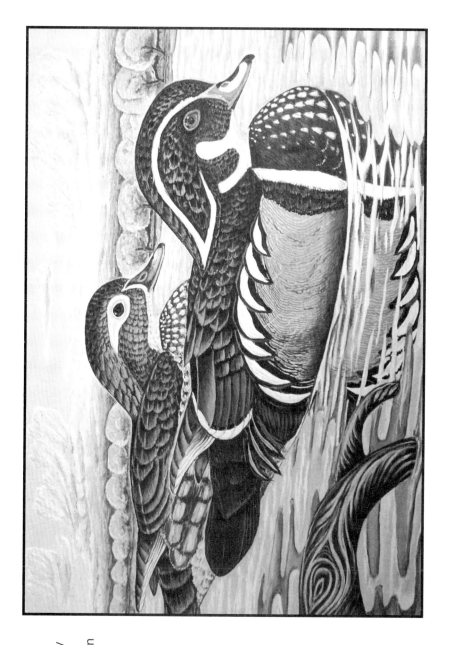

My 2003 Federal Duck Stamp Competition entry tied for sixteenth place and went on the national tour. I always place in the top twenty in the nation.

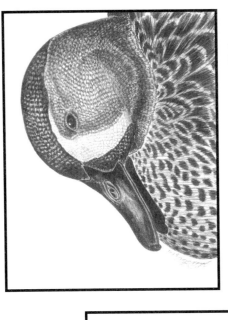

This blue-winged teal drawing was a gift for Iowa Governor Tom Vilsak.

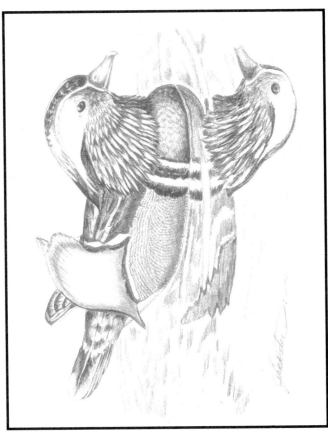

I drew this Mandarin Drake as a gift for Jerusalem's Mayor, Uri Lupolanski, when I was in Israel in October 2004.

Presenting Holocaust survivor Zev Kedem with a gift, April 2002 at the University of Wisconsin, Plattville. Zev is a lecturer, philosopher, writer, environmentalist, and documentary film producer. He also rebuilt Old Jerusalem after the 1967 war.

In Jerusalem, paying tribute at Oskar Schindler's grave site on October 7, 2004.

Right: My good friend, Yaakov Uri (far left), manager of ZAKA Rescue and Recovery, with ZAKA members and Prime Minister Ariel Sharon. *Below:* Yaakov with his son-in-law, Solomon.

In front of the Orthodox Christian Monastery, Kiev Pechersk Lavra, also called the Cave Monastery, founded in 1051 AD. The monastery is the preeminent center of Eastern Orthodox Christianity.

September 27, 2006, with Pastor Rick Schwendinger at the 65th Anniversary of the Babi-Yar Massacre.

The Children's Monument in Kiev brings remembrance of the tens of thousands of children who were murdered at Babi-Yar.

With my brother Mark, my sister Sharon, and my mom as Mark graduated from Coe College in 1988, "Magna Cum Laude." My mom overcame much adversity and did a tremendous job raising her five children.

In Kiev September 29, 2004, with Natan Gomberg, director of the Hesed in Kiev (they distribute four hundred thousand hot meals to elderly Jews in Kiev each year), and Evguene Shedkov, director of the Jewish Joint Distribution Committee.

In Yalta on the Black Sea with my fiancée, Victoria on September 23, 2007. This is the most recent photo of me. Many people would never guess I have been burned so badly. I praise the Lord for His restoration!

PART TWO

RECOVERY

The process of recovery often includes many trying nights. But the cry of your soul is heard by the Father. In these monumental times of transition, it is vital that you develop an intimate relationship with the Jewish Redeemer, Jesus Christ, and find fellowship with the Father by the power of the Holy Spirit.

> For he orders his angels to protect you wherever you go… For the Lord says, "Because he loves me, I will rescue him; I will make him great because he trusts in my name. When he calls on me I will answer; I will be with him in trouble, and rescue him and honor him. I will satisfy him with a full life and give him my salvation" (Ps. 91:11, 14-16).

During seasons of recovery, the greatest gift you can give yourself is to develop your relationship with the Lord in a more intimate way. You will be able to accomplish and overcome more than you ever would have believed! The Holy Spirit will give you courage to face the obstacles on your path and become victorious over all that has slowed your progress.

In these great times of earth-shaking transition, the dark clouds that were evident in your life will fade fast as the brilliant glory of God shines through you. Yes, you are a vessel that the Lord will greatly use! "Arise, My People! Let your light shine for all the nations to see! For the glory of the Lord is streaming from you" (Isa. 60:1).

■ ■ ■

CHAPTER FIVE

THE PROMISE

Moses, God's Gift to Humanity

There was nothing extraordinary about that morning. Moses arose before sunrise, as he had done for the last forty years, and prepared to spend another day shepherding the flocks of his aging father-in-law, Jethro. In the early darkness, Moses noticed how delightfully the desert finches and sunbirds sang as the chilly atmosphere turned from deep shades of purple to the golden, warm glow of predawn.

As the sun peeked over the Midian horizon, Moses wondered how his life could have been different. He felt a deep sense of mourning and an unspeakable emptiness because he could do nothing to help his people in Egypt. These were people he knew very little about. But in his heart, he had been drawn to the Hebrews even before he realized he was one of them. Many mornings, facing east, he would watch the sunrise with its brilliant scarlet-orange hues. In the stillness of his soul, he listened as the kaleidoscope-colored bee eaters sang their romantic love songs to each other across the valley. Looking west with questions in his heart, he could not help but wonder how his family was doing in

Egypt. Were his faithful and godly parents still alive? Had Aaron and Miriam survived the brutal taskmaster yet another day? These questions haunted his mind and stirred his heart. Sure, his life was less than he had expected and extremely difficult. But he was a free man in a foreign land that now called him friend.

That morning was the fifteenth of Nissan; it was spring. As Moses had faithfully done for forty years, he whispered a silent prayer that someday, somehow, his people would be free. As the shadows of the misty atmosphere gave way to the glowing hues of amber, he felt a new warmth and comfort in his soul. Moses' thoughts turned to the lambing season and the tasks that would consume his day. It was no more special than the rest—merely an average day in the twilight of Moses' life. However, this day would prove extraordinary, changing the course of history and generations of believers!

■ ■ ■

Troubled by the increasing population of the Hebrew slaves, Pharaoh had issued an order to kill all the infant boys in Goshen. During that time, a holy couple welcomed a beautiful son on 7 Adar, 1393 BCE. Amid the shadows of the tyrannical rule in Egypt, they hid their special son. Some eighty years later, their son was living a life of obscurity, unaware that he was about to change the course of history.

> One day as Moses was tending the flock of his father-in-law Jethro, the priest of Midian, out at the edge of the desert near Horeb, the mountain of God, suddenly the Angel of Jehovah appeared to him as a flame of fire in a bush. When Moses saw that the bush was on fire and that it didn't burn up, he went over to investigate. Then God called out to him, "Moses! Moses!" "Who is it?" Moses asked (Ex. 3:1-4).

The brilliance of that early morning sunrise could not compare with the beauty of the mysterious fire that captivated Moses' attention.

"Do not come any closer," God told him. "Take off your shoes, for you are standing on holy ground. I am the God of your fathers—the God of Abraham, Isaac, and Jacob." (Moses covered his face with his hands, for he was afraid to look at God.) (Ex. 3:5-6)

This was the extraordinary beginning of Moses' new life. There must have been real comfort in the tender parts of his heart, knowing that what God had planned for him would far exceed anything he could have done on his own, even if he had become ruler of Egypt. The reassurance that God had not forgotten this humble shepherd was amazing. God had not only remembered His friend Moses but also planned all along to use him to free the Hebrews. God had heard Moses' prayer to set the captives free, and Moses had become the answer to his own prayer. Yes, Moses was the yielded vessel God would use to liberate the Israelites from Pharaoh's grip.

Understandably awed and amazed, Moses stood very still as he contemplated this voice. His terror was tempered by the warm assurance that resonated from deep within his being. It was a voice from his past, calling him to a destiny established before he was born. A process of restoration began in the shepherd's soul as God revealed His plan.

In the sovereign awe of the moment, Moses couldn't help but wonder, *Why would God use me? I am old and don't speak well. Can't He find someone else?* Then the Lord revealed His assignment and gave him signs and wonders to perform for Pharaoh. The miracles gave the weathered shepherd courage to agree to the task and begin the amazing journey that would set a captive nation free. In doing so, Moses also became liberated with new vision and freedom!

With a clear sense of divine purpose and with the glory of God radiating from his face, Moses' spirit was renewed. Even the sheep seemed to have an awareness of God's presence! Deep in the wilderness of Sinai, the mountain of God, Moses was restored!

That night as Moses walked into the camp, a humble determination glistened in his eyes. He didn't need to say a word; the thrill of his conversation with God was evident on his face. His emotions must have been all over the place as he told Zipporah what had happened to him in the wilderness.

In all those forty years, Jethro had never seen Moses look like this. Sitting under the peaceful evening sky, with the flames from the campfire gently dancing to the rhythmic melody of the night, the two of them discussed Moses' encounter with God. Moses shared what the Lord had told him that day.

> I have seen the deep sorrows of my people in Egypt, and have heard their pleas for freedom from their harsh taskmasters. I have come to deliver them from the Egyptians and to take them out of Egypt into a good land, a large land "flowing with milk and honey"(Ex. 3:7-8).

Under the night sky, illuminated by a million stars, Jethro's soft eyes expressed his curiosity as Moses shared God's plan. Moses spoke with a purposeful whisper as he recounted how God had told him that he would deliver the Israelites.

> "What do you have there in your hand?" the Lord asked him. And he replied, "A shepherd's rod." "Throw it down on the ground," the Lord told him. So he threw it down—and it became a serpent, and Moses ran from it! Then the Lord told him, "Grab it by the tail!" He did, and it became a rod in his hand again! (Ex. 4:2-4).

Upon hearing this, Jethro knew God had a special plan for his son-in-law. So he blessed them, and Moses took his wife and two sons and headed for Egypt.

On the long journey, as he silently pondered all that had happened, Moses was full of questions. This humble band of travelers met Moses' brother, Aaron, in the wilderness, and they warmly embraced. Aaron made acquaintance with Zipporah and the others. "Moses told Aaron what God had said they must do, and what they were to say, and told him about the miracles they must do before Pharaoh" (Ex. 4:28).

Moses and Aaron returned to Egypt and gathered the leaders of Israel. After performing signs and wonders, the people accepted Moses as the messenger sent by God to deliver His captive children.

As God had instructed, Moses and Aaron then took their petition to the Pharaoh. He simply laughed at them and then doubled the workload for the Hebrew slaves. When the leaders of Israel learned of the added work, they turned against Moses. Moses would soon become accustomed to disfavor among the very nation he was sent to deliver.

Our hero then returned to the Lord to protest that the Pharaoh hadn't listened and had become even more brutal than before. He challenged God:

> Then Moses went back to the Lord. "Lord," he protested, "how can you mistreat your own people like this? Why did you ever send me, if you were going to do this to them? Ever since I gave Pharaoh your message, he has only been more and more brutal to them, and you have not delivered them at all!" "Now you will see what I shall do to Pharaoh," the Lord told Moses. "For he must be forced to let my people go; he will not only let them go, but will drive them out of his land!" (Ex. 5:22-6:1).

The Lord reminded Moses who he was dealing with—the God of Abraham, Isaac, and Jacob; the Lord God Almighty. He would be faithful to deliver His people into the land He had promised to Abraham. He would be their God, and they would be His people. (Maybe some of us need this reminder today!)

The Lord then told Moses and Aaron to make another presentation before the Pharaoh. God told Moses that He would make Moses like a god to Pharaoh. Moses would give the instructions from the Lord and Aaron would carry them out. Moses told Pharaoh that God wanted His people released from bondage, but Pharaoh's heart was hardened.

According to God's instruction, Aaron took Moses' staff and threw it down, and it became a snake. Pharaoh called in his wise men and magicians, and they also made snakes appear. However, Moses' snake swallowed up Pharaoh's.

The next morning, the Lord told Moses to approach Pharaoh as he bathed in the Nile. Once again Moses requested the release of the Israelites, and once again Pharaoh refused. As a display of God's sovereignty, Moses struck the water of the Nile with his staff, turning it to blood. Even the water in the bowls and pitchers set out for Pharaoh's bath turned to blood. This curse lasted for an entire week.

Once again, God told Moses to go before Pharaoh, requesting the release of his people. Stubborn Pharaoh still refused, even after a week with no pure water to drink. The result of his refusal was a plague of frogs, covering all of Egypt. Pharaoh slept with frogs in his bed and ate with frogs on his table, and still he refused to honor Moses' request. Pharaoh's magicians responded by making frogs appear from the earth, calling a double plague upon the people of Egypt.

Finally, Pharaoh called for Moses, asking him to pray to the God of the Hebrews, and, at last, the frogs died. They were gathered in to large piles, and the stench carried throughout the country. Can you imagine? However, Pharaoh's heart hardened once again, just as God had spoken to Moses.

Then the Lord instructed Moses to tell Aaron to strike his staff into the dust, turning the dust of Egypt to swarms of gnats. Pharaoh's magicians tried to do the same, but this time they failed. Gnats covered all of the people and animals. The magicians warned Pharaoh that this was the hand of God. But he still didn't listen.

The Lord instructed Moses to get up early in the morning when Pharaoh was at the Nile. This time he told him that if he didn't let God's people go to the wilderness to worship, the country would be plagued by flies, everywhere except the land of

Goshen (so that Pharaoh would know that God was protecting the Hebrews). However, once again Pharaoh hardened his heart, and "Jehovah did as he had said, so that there were terrible swarms of flies in the Pharaoh's palace and in every home in Egypt" (Ex. 8:24). Then Pharaoh repented briefly and called in Moses to stop the flies.

Yet another plague came upon Egypt for Pharaoh's refusal. This time, all of the livestock in Egypt died, but not one in the land of Goshen perished. Pharaoh still refused. God instructed Moses to take soot from a furnace and throw it into the air as Pharaoh watched, spreading it across all of Egypt, causing boils to appear on the people and animals. This time, the magicians were unable to stand before Moses because the boils had broken out upon them.

The Lord then instructed Moses to lift his hands toward the sky, and a great hail storm pelted Egypt. Never before had Egypt endured a storm of that magnitude. The hail killed livestock and every person who was caught in it. It shredded the trees and crops.

Next, the Lord sent swarming locusts that ate whatever crops had survived the hail. The ground was blackened with locusts. Not one crop remained untouched. In Goshen, however, they were spared all of these plagues.

Then the Lord sent a plague of darkness that lasted for three days and terrified all of Egypt. The people hardly moved, but in Goshen there was light, joy and laughter! Still, Pharaoh was unmoved.

"Then the Lord said to Moses, 'I will send just one more disaster on Pharaoh and his land, and after that he will let you go; in fact; he will be so anxious to get rid of you that he will practically throw you out of the country' " (Ex. 11:1).

On God's instruction, Moses told Pharaoh that at midnight the Lord would pass through Egypt, and the firstborn males, from the palace down to the commoner—even the firstborn male animals—would die. The Lord then instructed Moses to prepare his people for the first Passover. This is a celebration of the great power of Almighty God in delivering Israel. A branch of hyssop was dipped into the blood of a sacrificial lamb and the doorposts of God's chosen people were marked by the blood. This would cause the death angel to pass by.

This night of terror in Egypt did not touch a single Hebrew. But the story has a different ending for the Egyptians. Pharaoh had once decreed that all the firstborn of the Hebrews would die. This had unleashed God's fury against the oppressor, and Pharaoh's own words had become a death sentence for Egypt. Pharaoh even lost his pride and joy, his firstborn son.

When this night of terror was over, Pharaoh allowed the captive Hebrews their freedom.

That very night, after the Passover Feast, the children of Israel left Ramses and started for Succoth. It was 15 Nissan 2448 (counting from the time of creation on the Jewish calendar). God had orchestrated this move on the very last day of Israel's four hundred and thirtieth year in Egypt. I can only imagine the awe and inspired joy that the Hebrews must have felt as they left for their Promised Land, taking with them the gold, silver and treasures of Egypt. They also took with them the bones of Joseph, who had been promised a burial with his people. Their freedom was evidence of the covenant promise God Almighty had made with Joseph's great-grandfather, Abraham.

There were six hundred thousand men between the ages of twenty and sixty. Jewish scholars have estimated that the entire exodus population was between two and three million people! Imagine the size of this nation moving out of Egypt! It was comparable to the population of Houston, Manhattan, or Chicago! If the Great Wall of China can be seen from the moon, so too could this great mass exodus have been seen from space! With great power, the God of Abraham had delivered His children.

Then Moses said to the people, "This is a day to remember forever—
the day of leaving Egypt and your slavery; for the Lord has brought
you out with mighty miracles. Now remember, during the annual
celebration of this event you are to use no yeast; don't even have any
in your homes" (Ex. 13:3).

Great joy was heard that night as they left their place
of bondage with the wealth of Egypt. The restoration of
Israel had begun!

◼ ◼ ◼

Any time you are in a process of recovery in your life, God
will open doors of opportunity for you. Look at Moses, who
at the age of eighty thought his life was forgotten. Instead, with
great wisdom God opened wide the doors of heaven and used
Moses to recover the covenant that He had made with His friend
Abraham. All you have to do is trust God and be obedient. If
you happen to miss it, like Moses did occasionally, then simply
ask for forgiveness and move forward with great boldness!

Often when we find ourselves in a situation that feels like
prison to us, we are being prepared for a greater calling. We are
being delivered from great oppression and injustice into God's
liberty and freedom. Times of trials are excellent training grounds
for the greater heights that God wants to take His people to.
When I have gone through injustices and delayed promises, I
have wondered what it was all about. One time the Lord spoke
to me, "This is all a training ground." I later found out that in the
midst of my trials and disappointments, God was training me for
something much higher—His promise for my life. He wants the
same for your life. Expect great things; God wants us to think
big, dream big, and accomplish great things as we live under His
guidance and as we are directed by His Glory!

◼ ◼ ◼

PRAYER OF ENCOURAGEMENT: Father, God of Abraham, I ask that you help your people as they go through periods of transition. Please cover them! Give them the wisdom to see the whole picture and not look at their current circumstances. Father, I ask that you equip your saints with power from the Holy Spirit to endure the changes that are rapidly occurring in their life! Give them exceeding courage in the next move of God. Father, you protect your people during the recovery process! I ask that this prayer be sealed in the hearts of those reading, that they may know that you are going to use them greatly! I ask this in the blood of the Lamb of God, the eternal atonement, Jesus the Messiah! Seal it with your power, Lord! Amen!

CHAPTER SIX

BEAUTY FOR ASHES

The Road to Recovery Begins

I recall the drive home from Iowa City. It was a warm, beautifully sunny October day. My mother and grandmother picked me up from the hospital. I felt like a free person who had just been liberated from captivity. I had not been outside the hospital in almost two months. I noticed the beauty of everything. It seemed like I was seeing the world for the very first time. I vividly recall feeling like I had been blind and had suddenly regained my vision. I also remember how hot the sun felt on my very tender skin. I had been warned to stay out of the sun because I would be affected by hot and cold temperatures. (Most of my oil glands were destroyed in the inferno. These are what keep your body temperature regulated.)

I was alive and full of hope and optimism! My heart song was "This is the day the Lord has made. We will rejoice and be glad in it" (Ps. 118:24). But I was beginning a journey that would include many difficulties, just like the journey of Israel. They had so much hope and joy as they entered their opportunity for freedom. Yet there were many difficulties ahead of them.

As I arrived home, the first thing I saw was the huge "Welcome Home John" banner that was stretched across the front of the house. My dog, Uncle Rags, had missed me, and I was surprised that he recognized me. I must have looked like a shell of my former self, nearly fifty pounds lighter.

I always walked deliberately, careful not to injure my painful right arm, which was protected by a sling. My healing skin was very tender and itched badly. I had been told not to scratch, but it was just too much, even with the medication I was given. I developed "nerve blisters" (my own term) from rubbing against the door frame to relieve the itching. The blisters became painful and my mother would use a syringe to remove the fluid from them.

Before long, I began my routine of physical therapy sessions at the nearby Virginia Gay Hospital. My therapy routine would continue for the next three and a half years. I was scheduled five times a week the first year, three times a week the second, and twice a week the third. I became sick and tired of this routine, but, unfortunately, the rehabilitation process is lengthy.

My advice to anyone in recovery of any kind is to just take one day at a time. Don't examine the process too closely. You won't be able to see the whole picture, and the prospect may overwhelm you. Keep your eyes on Jesus and let the love of God sustain you. Concentrate on the greater appreciation and fuller perspective you have gained. Set your mind on hopeful things, and you will discover God's mercy and faithfulness at a new level.

I began the visits to outpatient physical therapy with a lot of uncertainty and apprehension. I couldn't drive, nor could I use my hands in any functional way. My journey to the department, which was down a long hallway and down a flight of stairs, was met with curious stares from staff members who had heard of my situation. I was still bandaged and moved slowly, so this was a tedious process.

My hair had been cropped very short to minimize the risk of infection in the unhealed tissue at the tops of my ears. I wore a blue jogging outfit that contrasted with my bright red complexion. Sue, my physical therapist, was a little unsettled by seeing me. I don't think she had realized what she had gotten herself into when she accepted me as a patient. Sue's assistant, Ethel Morillo, was a willing and cheerful individual. Together, the three of us applied generous doses of humor to every situation. Ethel loved everyone, especially God. She had a hard life but was extremely kind to everyone she met. We remained friends until her death, some sixteen years later.

That first day of treatment was an experience in adjustment. It was so important to get into the whirlpool each morning. My circulation was very poor; I had lost many of the oil glands in my skin, and these are vital for regulating body temperature. My arm was still in the sling, and it was so painful. When I had to remove it from the sling and place it in the water, there was a sharp pain that was almost heart-stopping.

The first session was short because our expectations were limited and we all had to get used to this way of life. I was very skinny, tired and ready to head home. Looking back, I am very grateful for the people who loved me through that outrageously turbulent time.

Due to the fact I had been discharged from the Burn Unit early, I still had weekly visits at the University. The drive to Iowa City was about ninety minutes. I became accustomed to long periods of waiting, and then testing, and then waiting. There was preparation for additional surgeries and procedures. This accident had definitely changed my life, and it was up to me and my family to re-establish some sort of normalcy. The journey to recovery was a lonely one, and some days were very sad. For my mother there was the burden of transporting me to all of my appointments. Thank God, she was extremely devoted and did everything possible to make my recovery process a success. However, those weekly pilgrimages to Iowa City exhausted me.

Sue had heard of a treatment for burn patients developed at Mayo Clinic. It seems a surgeon was traveling the back roads of Minnesota during a blizzard when his vehicle went into a ditch. He was stranded in a remote area, and the wind chill was dangerously below zero. He set out to find help and came upon a farmhouse eventually, but not before suffering severe frostbite. He was painfully aware of what this would mean for his career as a surgeon; he would potentially lose his fingers, and at the least he would suffer loss of dexterity. He was invited into the farmhouse, and the woman who lived there quickly went to work treating his hands. Her home remedy of Vaseline and aloe vera had been effective for many burns and abrasions, and soon she had mixed them into a mint-colored whip.

When skin has been burned, there is a loss of seven types of sugar from the tissues. Apparently, aloe vera contains all seven sugars. This wise woman applied the mixture liberally to the doctor's frostbite. Over a period of days, the doctor was astounded to realize his fingers had regained their color.

Sue learned that this home remedy was being utilized in the treatment of burn patients. I thank God because she did her research.

Another common secondary complication for burn patients is pneumonia. Due to the body's inability to regulate temperature, many patients die from pneumonia. It became evident that my love of the outdoors would have to be approached with great caution. This was particularly sad during autumn, which was not only my favorite time of year but also the painful anniversary of the explosion.

Therapy sessions were part of my daily routine. Sue worked to keep my arm and fingers flexible by stretching the tissues, which was painful. They told me in the Burn Unit that skin is similar to a rubber band and that it's necessary to continually stretch the scarred areas to keep the skin from shrinking. This process takes years.

Ethel would be in charge of mixing up the aloe vera and Vaseline concoction. She would cheerfully hum a tune to herself as she whipped the ingredients together. After a few minutes in the whirlpool, I endured the stretching necessary. Then the aloe mixture was heavily applied to the burnt areas. After the mixture dried, it was time for the "fun" process of getting the tan-colored Jobst pressure outfit on!

A Jobst is a heavy, woven nylon garment the size of a three-year-old's shirt (remember I'm six feet two inches tall). It was intentionally small to maintain pressure on the scars as they healed. At first, the hardest part was getting my right arm into the Jobst. I was completely helpless and my arm was so painful. I was so skinny that I could almost feel my left thumb with my left forefinger as I placed them between the two bones of my right arm. It was the size of a child's arm. I had become very protective of my arm so nothing touched it. And from time to time the arm would go numb (as it still occasionally does). The episodes of numbness are so painful that it is often difficult to breathe.

The day in, day out process of therapy was frustrating, but I knew it was important. It kept me moving forward, one tiny step at a time. The scarring began to create webbing between my fingers, so Sue applied extra pieces of foam between them before the Jobst gloves were put on. Once when she was applying the aloe whip she said, "John, I can't believe it—your skin is so dry that it absorbs the aloe like a sponge!"

My therapy required a lot of that mixture in the five years of treatment, but it greatly aided my healing process. At my mom's suggestion, I also began taking a lot of strong vitamins. When I visited the University for routine checkups, the doctors and nurses would marvel at how quickly I was healing! I told them about the aloe mixture, but they weren't interested in hearing about it because it was from Mayo Clinic! Normally each university wants to come up with its own ideas. At that time, the University of Iowa was using shark oil for burn treatments.

(Today they use other oils, like emu.) So they were not interested in aloe treatment, but it really works. I am living proof!

I was fortunate to have a faith-filled family that would stand with me during this very difficult time. Because of the accident, my faith in Jesus became stronger and the bond within my family grew as well. We had been abandoned before, so we knew we needed to stand together. My mother had taught us the very important lessons of life and determined faith, which helped us excel in several areas of our lives.

On one of my visits to the University of Iowa I had an appointment with the Prosthetics Department. Anne Fyler was the head prosthetist. Her specialty was making pressure masks for burn patients in order to keep the burned tissue flattened, reducing scarring. The process involved lying back with cotton in my nostrils to keep the mold material out. I was required to breathe through a straw. It was an uncomfortable process that seemed to take forever. As the strips of plaster were applied and hardened, the chemical reaction caused them to become hot. Fortunately, the first impression was a good one. Using this casting as a mold, Anne fashioned a white plastic mask of my face without the scars. I was required to wear this mask over the next few years and spent a lot of time at home as a result. The first night I wore it I momentarily stopped breathing. It fit very tightly to my face, secured with straps, with only a small opening for my mouth.

Another phase of my recovery process was a series of steroid injections. These slowed the healing of my scars, allowing time for the face mask to flatten them. A local physician administered cortisone shots into my facial wounds with very tiny needles. The cortisone was the consistency of thick, white glue and burned as it was injected, often making me cry. There were over one hundred and twenty needle marks on my face, but this was another very effective treatment.

Receiving the injections and faithfully wearing the mask brought great results. Most people who meet me today don't know I've had over 68 percent of my body burned. I was recently in Kiev, Ukraine at Pastor Sunday Adelaja's church. I spoke to six thousand people at a conference about the accident and overcoming adversity. My interpreter told me he was shocked to learn that I had been burned so severely. So I thank God for my healing!

■ ■ ■

Before my accident, I had been making plans to attend taxidermy school. I was interested in studying the structure, detail, and anatomy of animals. I felt that this would help me become a better wildlife artist. If it worked for John Audubon and Maynard Reece (record five-time winner of the Federal Duck Stamp Competition), then it would work for me. I had one minor delay—it was called an "explosion!"

With courage and a hopeful spirit, I went off to Wisconsin for taxidermy school. It had only been nine months since my injury. I had only 60 percent use of my right arm, and the fingers on my left hand were clumsy. I could not hold onto things. I was still going through the daily process and the setbacks of physical therapy, but it was time to press into my future. I knew the training phase of taxidermy school would be good physical therapy, and I couldn't afford to lose the use of my hands. I soon learned the introductory taxidermy skills, but frustration was ever-present as I learned to use my clumsy left hand.

■ ■ ■

I will praise the Lord no matter what happens. I will constantly speak of his glories and grace. I will boast of all his kindness to me. Let all who are discouraged take heart... For I cried to him and he answered me! He freed me from all my fears... For the Angel of the Lord guards and rescues all who reverence him (Ps. 34:1-7).

When you find yourself in a state of change or transition, the question is this: what do you do with the sense of displacement and loss? (The situation doesn't have to be as physically traumatic as mine. Your trial may be a divorce, the death of a loved one, or losing the job you thought would be yours for life.) It is difficult, but not impossible, to recover in these situations. You may feel that your life has been taken from you, that your destiny has gone in a direction you didn't plan. But what are you going to do? What will you say to people who ask, "How can you survive this?"

These are the seasons in which your foundation in Christ is vital. Your faith is being tested, and your life has become a witness, all at the same time. My advice is to keep trusting in the Lord. Isaiah 41:13 promises, "I am holding you by your right hand—I the Lord your God—and I say to you, Don't be afraid; I am here to help you."

When I reflect on my recovery process, I realize how important my faith was. It was truly a time of drawing close to God and knowing my Savior, Jesus, at a deeper level. God's grace allowed me to become closer to God, not more distant, and this saved me in the long run.

> For the Lord says, "Because he loves me, I will rescue him; I will make him great because he trusts in my name. When he calls on me I will answer; I will be with him in trouble, and rescue him and honor him. I will satisfy him with a full life and give him my salvation" (Ps. 91:14-16).

I certainly had an opportunity to be discouraged; my hopes and dreams were set aside while I watched everyone else move forward. I felt forgotten and forsaken. However, the Word always answered,

> But as for you, O Israel, you are mine, my chosen ones; for you are Abraham's family, and he was my friend. I have called you back from

the ends of the earth and said that you must serve but me alone, for I have chosen you and will not throw you away. Fear not, for I am with you. Do not be dismayed. I am your God. I will strengthen you; I will help you; I will uphold you with my victorious right hand (Isa. 41:8-10).

The psalmist speaks encouragement from the heart as he says,

The Heavens are telling of the glory of God; they are a marvelous display of his craftsmanship. Day and night they keep telling about God. Without a sound or word, silent in the skies, their message reaches out to all the world. The sun lives in the heavens where God placed it and moves out across the skies as radiant as a bridegroom going to his wedding, or as joyous as an athlete looking forward to a race! (Ps. 19:1-5).

■ ■ ■

PRAYER OF ENCOURAGEMENT: Father, I ask that you show your people special favor and give them moments of intimacy with you as they proceed on the road to recovery. Hide them in your shadow and protect them as they heal, just as you provided the Israelites with a pillar of fire in the night and a cloud in the daytime. Father, send special angels to guide and protect your people as they go on this journey. Send the power of the Holy Spirit to give comfort, counsel and wisdom in this process. I ask this in Jesus' name.

Chapter Seven

Recovering the Promise

A Corporate Promotion at Eighty

Don't be surprised if God asks you to do something great in the later years of your life. You know it's impossible by your own energy, but that's what God loves to do—display His strength through yielded vessels. He sent a man who had been groomed as a prince of Egypt into the wilderness for forty years with about three million rebellious people! At the age of eighty, Moses felt he had been forgotten. Yet in his new commission he was going to have a far greater impact than if he had become ruler of Egypt. God had called this humble servant to change the world.

But I have witnesses, O Israel, says the Lord! You are my witnesses and my servants, chosen to know and to believe me and to understand that I alone am God. There is no other God; there never was and never will be. I am the Lord, and there is no other Savior. Whenever you have thrown away your idols, I have shown you my power. With one word I have saved you. You have seen me do it; you are my witnesses that it is true. From eternity to eternity I am God. No one can oppose what I do (Isa. 43:10-13).

No more than a week into their jubilant march to freedom, the children of Israel realized that they were being pursued by the elite militia of Pharaoh's army. "So Pharaoh led the chase in his chariot, followed by the pick of Egypt's chariot corps—600 chariots in all—and other chariots driven by Egyptian officers" (Ex. 14:6-7). (The modern day equivalent would be the thundering sound of a well-equipped six hundred-member Humvee fleet, emerging from clouds of dust, chasing an unarmed group of refugees in the desert. It would be a terrifying scene.)

Pharaoh's approaching army caused panic among the people. Once again, the Israelites turned their doubt and fear toward Moses, complaining that he had brought them out of captivity and into the desert to die. "But Moses told the people, 'Don't be afraid. Just stand where you are and watch, and you will see the wonderful way the Lord will rescue you today. The Egyptians you are looking at—you will never see them again'" (Ex. 14:13).

Then the Lord told Moses to get moving. He told him to raise his staff over the water, convincing the people that they would walk across on dry ground. He told Moses that He would harden the hearts of the Egyptians and that they would follow Israel into the sea. Furthermore, God told Moses He would receive great glory at the expense of the Egyptian armies and that all of Egypt would know He is the Lord!

Then the Angel of the Lord positioned Himself between the nation of Israel and the Egyptian army as they traveled. As night fell, the pillar of cloud that had guided them through the day turned to a pillar of fire. However, it became darkness to the Egyptians and they could not find the Israelites. You'd think this would have caused terror among the Egyptians, but God had hardened their hearts to their own doom.

Moses lifted his hands toward the sea, and the Lord sent a strong east wind, opening a path for the Israelites to cross. By morning, the Egyptians had followed them into the dry seabed. One can only imagine the sobering fear that gripped the hearts of the Israelites as they faced Pharaoh's elite forces. At the time, the Egyptians were the most powerful nation on Earth. The Lord looked down from the pillar of fire and sent confusion into the Egyptian camp. Their chariot wheels began to fall off, and the army was frightened. "'Let's get out of here,' the Egyptians yelled. 'Jehovah is fighting for them and against us.'" (Ex. 14:25).

All of Israel was safe on the other side. Then the Lord told Moses to raise his hands to the sea once again. The waters that had parted to allow safe passage for the Israelites and entry for the pursuing army rushed back to the banks of the sea. Immediately, the ranks of Pharaoh's finest were consumed in a watery grave. God had proven faithful once again, and joyful shouts rang through the Hebrew camp. Those who had complained and grumbled against Moses were overcome with reverent fear.

■ ■ ■

God intended to adhere to the covenant He had made with Abraham. He was accomplishing this with Moses' obedience in leading God's people out of bondage. Often, the road to freedom takes twists and turns we don't anticipate. This may be the result of our unwillingness to submit to God's ways during our wilderness experiences. We must have a heart of unrestrained trust in God and willingness to cooperate with the deliverer He sends. Scripture shows the frequent complaining and bitterness that the children of Israel displayed during their many years in the wilderness. God knew a direct route to the "Promised Land" wouldn't have been effective in changing the rebellious ways of His people. He sovereignly knew what it would take to strengthen and prepare them for the opposition they had yet to face.

God told Israel that He would let them have the land little by little as they proved they could handle the responsibility and ownership of it. (It is like a person who rents most of his life and then decides to buy a home. This is a good decision, but the buyer is sometimes shocked by the responsibility that ownership entails. There is no landlord to complain to. Now he's responsible for everything.) Four hundred and thirty years of slavery did not prepare the Hebrews for the enormous responsibility of ownership.

■ ■ ■

Moses led Israel away from the Red Sea and into the Shur Desert. They traveled for three days in the desert and found no water. When they arrived at Marah they found water, but it was bitter. Once again, the people turned against Moses. God instructed Moses to throw a tree branch into the water. This prophetic act made the water drinkable. It was at Marah that the Lord laid out the conditions that would test their faith: "If you will listen to the voice of the Lord your God, and obey it, and do what is right, then I will not make you suffer the diseases I sent on the Egyptians, for I am the Lord who heals you" (Ex. 15:26).

A month after leaving Egypt, Moses led the children of Israel into the Sinai Desert between Elim and Mount Sinai. Again, the children of Israel complained bitterly against Moses and Aaron. So the Lord fed the multitude with manna and quail.

One thing we must all learn following a trying experience is to remain positive and not to get bitter. When we allow bitterness to creep into our life, it tarnishes what we could have learned through the trial. Bitterness consumes our future when we can't let go of the past. It steals our health, our time, our freedom, and our joy. But when we remain positive, God restores everything we think was lost.

Marah, the "bitter water," is just where the Israelites found themselves. If you find yourself at the bitter waters, don't remain there. Instead, look to God as your source of hope and joy. This eases the time spent in the deserts of life. The psalmist's prayer says it best;

O Lord our God, the majesty and glory of your name fills all the earth and overflows the heavens. You have taught the little children to praise you perfectly. May their example shame and silence your enemies! When I look up into the night skies and see the work of your fingers— the moon and the stars you have made—I cannot understand how you can bother with mere puny man, to pay any attention to him! And yet you have made him only a little lower than the angels, and placed a crown of glory and honor upon his head. You have put him in charge of everything you made; everything is put under his authority: all sheep and oxen, and wild animals too, the birds and fish, and all the life in the sea. O Jehovah, our Lord, the majesty and glory of your name fills the earth (Ps. 8:1-9).

It was exactly two months after the Lord delivered the Israelites out of the hand of Pharaoh that He spoke to Moses on Mount Sinai.

Give these instructions to the people of Israel. Tell them, "You have seen what I did to the Egyptians, and how I brought you to myself as though on eagle's wings. Now if you will obey me and keep your part of my contract with you, you shall be my own little flock from among all the nations of the earth; for all the earth is mine. And you shall be a kingdom of priests to God, a holy nation" (Ex. 19:3-6).

The laws God gave Moses were intended to protect His people from harmful behaviors and diseases. They outlined the conduct that enabled the Jewish people to remain safe (providing they were not persecuted) and to live lives of integrity. (During several historical outbreaks of disease, Jews came under suspicion due to their superior health; following God's standards of hygiene made them less susceptible even to the Black Plague!) Many great nations, including the United States, have based their constitution upon the foundation of God's law.

During the forty years in the desert, Moses had many face to face encounters and became a friend of God—the same privilege that Abraham had enjoyed. Canaan was to be the re-establishment of God's covenant with Abraham. The Canaanites had defiled themselves with sexual sins and were expelled from the land. Leviticus 18:27 says, "Yes, all these abominations have been done continually by the people of the land where I am taking you, and the land is defiled."

The Lord originally intended that the children of Israel take the land, not that they allow the fear of the unknown to hinder their progress. However, we know the story of the twelve scouts who were sent into the enemy's camp. Only two returned with good news: Joshua from the tribe of Ephraim (Joseph's oldest son born in Egypt), and Caleb from the tribe of Judah (the tribe of the line of King David and Jesus Christ). The remaining ten scouts brought doubt and fear to the hearts of the people, saying that the inhabitants were too big to overtake. So recovery of the promise took longer than what God had planned. I believe that if the children of Israel had trusted God, He would have destroyed the enemies of Israel like He did the Egyptian army. Years later, Rahab told Joshua's two spies,

> We are all afraid of you; everyone is terrified if the word *Israel* is even mentioned. For we have heard how the Lord made a path through the Red Sea for you when you left Egypt! …No wonder we are afraid of you! No one has any fight left in him after hearing things like that, for your God is the supreme God of heaven, not just an ordinary god (Josh. 2:9,11).

It is up to us during these times of transition to continue going forward with the Lord's plan. We must not look at our current circumstances; they're just a smokescreen from the enemy. The reality is this: the Lord will go ahead of you and win the battle for you. The battle is the Lord's.

When the Lord restores a promise, it will be a complete restoration. We must patiently trust His timing and His purposes, not taking matters into our own hands. God sees the whole picture. We do not. Times like these are tender opportunities to grow in faith and humility. God says, "I refresh the humble and give new courage to those with repentant hearts" (Isa. 57:15).

As He did with Moses, God will use you in the recovery of your promise. Do not let your age, level of education, or health keep you from pressing into the realms where God wants to move you. Pray for understanding and wisdom in each issue you face. Don't be surprised or overcome by opposition. It may look as if there are giants in the land, but press in to the truth of the Word. Fear will only hinder your progress, stunting your Christian growth. God is faithful to His specific promise for your life. Remember, Moses was given a corporate promotion at eighty! God will also do great things in your life. These great things will happen when maturity outweighs impulsiveness and human weakness is replaced with God's power and anointing on your life. "Understand, therefore, that the Lord your God is the faithful God who for a thousand generations keeps his promises and constantly loves those who love him and obey his commands" (Deut. 7:9).

■ ■ ■

PRAYER OF ENCOURAGEMENT: Father of love, Father of light, God of eternal promises, I ask that you help your people step into the realm of your promises for their lives. Father God, please endow your people with the hearts of servants. Watch over them as they journey towards their promise. Father, in Jesus' name, confuse the enemy's attempts to derail them on their journey. Give your angels of mercy charge over your chosen ones. Guide and protect them on their road to recovery. I ask that these pathways of truth become evident, directing each step with wisdom. In Jesus' precious name I pray.

CHAPTER EIGHT

DAYS OF LIGHT, MOMENTS OF HOPE

Healing Your Memories

One of the greatest gifts we can receive is the healing of our memories. Often, when a tragic event occurs, we are swept away by the activity of the recovery process. We just try to survive moment by moment, and we frequently omit the process of emotional healing.

I pray that God will give you wisdom, understanding, and an anointing to heal the issues in your life. Only by the power of the Holy Spirit are deep issues of pain revealed to us. As they are brought into the light, true healing can take place. In this chapter we'll explore the journey of hope and some of the strategies God has given me to effectively complete the process of my recovery. I am confident God will do the same in your life, imparting His power and providing you with peace of mind.

When we experience trying times, we tend to lose perspective of the blessings in our lives. It's important to take inventory of the goodness in our life so that hopelessness does not overtake us. Following the explosion, it was sometimes difficult to maintain an attitude of thanksgiving. There I was, just nineteen years old. Before that fateful day, my future looked bright and promising. However, I was painfully aware that I was now facing a long road to recovery. In times like that, we should allow ourselves the freedom to focus on one day at a time, trusting God for every step.

Once I accepted my situation and drew near to God, I grew incredibly because I had chosen not to get bitter. Others have walked this path before me, and their inspiration and example has strengthened many. Christopher Reeve's courage greatly inspired me in recent years. On October 10, 2004, I was in Jerusalem when I heard the news that he had died. It made me so sad, but through adversity he had truly become "Superman" and inspired millions, including me.

I've found that there is a deepening of our relationship with the Lord that can only happen when faced with the devastation of a loss or tragedy. In those moments, we may feel set-aside. However, when Jesus shows up and imparts His nature to us, we realize that He is really all that matters. Trust the Word. God has a bigger plan for your life. I can not over-emphasize this point: God's comfort and protection for you is released when you daily bathe in His presence and light. You will be restored to a great ability and a more powerful God-oriented focus on the unlimited "promises" for your life. God will nurture us in the womb of His love and heal us during these times when we feel that we have been overlooked. The work that the Lord is doing in us is a far greater work than we realize or understand. This focus will bring you through the tough times when the pain is relentless and you watch everyone else go on with their life while you cannot.

■ ■ ■

I knew from the time I was twelve years old that God was going to use me to bless the nation of Israel. That knowledge gave me the courage to live just one more day. I knew I had been sidetracked, but I also knew that God was still on His throne! I sit here today, absolutely amazed, as I realize that God's promises for my life will bear great fruit for Israel! The Lord has recently shown me one way to accomplish this through long-term financial planning, through a charitable trust I recently established. And I stand humbly amazed that recently I was given an "open invitation" to meet any of the leaders of Israel that I want to. I praise God for fulfilled promises! This journey has been thirty-three years in the making. God's timing is always perfect!

■ ■ ■

In my life there have been many difficult situations. So I remember thinking to myself during the explosion, *Well, here we go again!*

At that time I was the head of my household and had four dependents. I was young but mature beyond my years. My mother had almost died from ovarian cancer when I was eight years old. Her weight dropped to about eighty-five pounds following a course of chemotherapy—it devastated her health. In the midst of her illness she underwent surgery and died twice on the operating table. She also suffered a miscarriage, losing her youngest daughter.

My mother's only support system at this time was her father, and he died unexpectedly. A cemetery plot was purchased for her when she was only thirty-five years old. Plans were being made to distribute her children among the relatives, but it seemed that none of our relatives wanted my brother Mark and I, so we were scheduled to be sent to an orphanage.

However, God had other plans. With His glorious power He restored my mother to health. She received the baptism of the Holy Spirit, and so did her children! Our lives changed incredibly from that point on. My parents had been separated for five years, but Dad officially left us during this time—he didn't want the responsibility of his family any longer. We were required to sell our beautiful home and downsize to a mobile home in the country. Mom was full of faith in the Lord, however, and she walked in love, obedience, and humility!

By faith my mother moved her young family to the rural countryside of Garner, Iowa. That change in atmosphere enabled me to nurture my love for nature. I spent hours hunting and exploring, and in the process I grew as a nature artist.

At the encouragement of my art teacher, I submitted an entry to a large regional art show when I was just fifteen. To my surprise, my entry took the show. I not only received the "Peoples Choice Award" but also "Grand Champion." When I was sixteen, I submitted an entry in my first Iowa Duck, Trout and Habitat Stamp Competition. My plans for my future were hopeful and in motion.

■ ■ ■

As I write this chapter, the Lord is reminding me how important inner healing is and how that truth was impressed upon me by His Holy Spirit. If your trial has caused you to doubt who you are in Christ or who He is as your Healer, take time to pursue healing.

Know this: the Lord loves you. He also wants *you* to love who you are and become the incredible person that He specifically created you to be during this historic time on earth. We can not be perfect in our own power, but only with God by our side every step of the way. He transforms us into excellent vessels of humble, yet powerful, maturity. Then there is complete joy for us as we walk with the determined focus of our eternal importance.

The Lord brought this lesson home to me several years ago. We had a goose on our farm that was hit by a car. He limped for a period of time, but then his injury healed. The interesting thing is that even though he completely recovered, he continued to limp as if the wound were fresh. In the goose's mind he was still crippled. In the same way, we often continue to limp emotionally after surviving a painful circumstance. When we go through an event or a trauma but don't renew our minds, we can continue to react as if the injury just happened.

It is so important to pursue healing of painful memories. The Lord showed me that it's possible to heal our memories of an event that happened many years ago. When the core issue of our pain is exposed, it can be dealt with as we allow Jesus to speak.

We all have issues that can potentially hinder our progress in becoming all God has created us to be. Whatever the issue, if it's holding you back, I encourage you to pursue healing.

One thing I learned while recovering from my injuries was that I had unhealed issues of abandonment, loneliness and fear from my childhood. Ignoring my pain didn't mean it had been dealt with. I tried, with great effort, to just "get over" the wounds from my past. However, as my mother always said, ignoring your issues only causes the problems to "take on a life of their own."

Whatever your issue is, don't be afraid to confront it head-on. In the grace of God, there is healing and restoration from past wounds. That's why Jesus went to Calvary. He didn't want us to be partially saved, healed or delivered, but to walk in the fullness of all He accomplished. Maybe you were abandoned when you were young and you've struggled with rejection. Begin by acknowledging your true feelings. We often spend a lot of time trying to reject our feelings because we don't know what to do with them. Allow the Lord to minister to you in your pain. His truth will set you free.

■ ■ ■

PRAYER OF ENCOURAGEMENT: Father, in Jesus' name, I ask that you release those who are hurting and bearing wounds from past experiences. You know the path they've been on, Lord, and you are the Mighty Healer of everything that holds us back. Lord, please clearly reveal the issues to your children and assure them your love is a safe place to rest. Set us free from all that keeps us from your glory, in the mighty name of Jesus! Amen.

PART THREE

RESTORATION

Whenever a situation causes upheaval or change in the course of your life, remember that God is there to help you. There are three phases of a major life-changing event. The first phase is **the traumatic event** itself. It could be an illness, an injury, the loss of a loved one, or a financial crisis. The second phase is the process of **recovery and healing**. This stage is a day-to-day, moment-by-moment restoration process. Critical growth happens in this stage, and it is a precious time of intimate revelation of God's love and sufficiency. Seek to find your rest in Him. The third phase is **restoration**. Even though it may seem hard to believe from your present vantage point, your trust in the Lord will bear fruit.

In this section I'll be focusing on the restoration phase, what God has done in my life, and—more importantly—what He will do in your life. God has many promises to fulfill in your life. He will give you the power and wisdom to accomplish all that He has anointed you to do. God has done many miracles in my life and has placed me in a position to be used by Him. This includes a special connection with Israel.

God hears our prayers and feels the anguish we experience very deeply. He is ultimately compassionate and merciful. Too many people give up in the second phase of their trial, growing weary of the battle. This is a pivotal time to press in to the truth we find in the Word for our strength and to proclaim our deliverance prophetically in agreement. When everything looks impossible, God is most glorified. Discover Him in the midst of your difficulty.

■ ■ ■

CHAPTER NINE

VISIONS AND ANGELS

Spiritual Gifts to Encourage You

God sends His angels to protect His people. Some of the fortunate have actually seen angelic beings. Angels are very real and have been reported to be present in many perilous situations. It would be difficult to know all that angels do for us, but they are mentioned in Scripture forty-four times. There are at least fourteen angelic appearances in the Old Testament and thirteen in the New Testament. It's important to remember that angels are God's messengers, sent in response to our prayers. (They are not to be the focus of our prayers, however.) In this chapter, I would like to share about some angelic encounters in my own life.

During my recovery and rehabilitation, several people heard that I had gone to school for taxidermy and asked me to do mounting projects for them. This began on a small scale, part-time, and proved to be a very effective means of therapy for my hands. It also provided much-needed income for my mother, brother, and sisters.

It was a critical economic time for the entire Midwest; the "Farm Crisis" was in full swing. To be starting a business in the midst of a critical financial depression may have seemed foolish. I was helping support my brother and sisters with college expenses and had also put a down payment on a farm. The overall situation was extremely difficult for me emotionally, and it seemed I was watching my life pass me by without seeing my dreams fulfilled. But the Lord helped me realize that the difficult trials in life are times for great growth.

A key principle is to see your life with an eternal perspective, not just through your current circumstances. When you are experiencing a great trial or difficulty, it is important to stay focused on what God is doing in your life. The battles may be daily and the setbacks may be many, but with purposeful diligence you can overcome a tragic event, emerging with an incredible testimony and a newly acquired skill that will be priceless in helping others who face similar trials.

■ ■ ■

With joy I started my business July 4, 1985, calling it Red Fox Studio. In the first year of business, my workload increased 500 percent. Anyone who has studied business knows that the first five years of any business are referred to as "the night terrors." Will you succeed? Will people like what you do? Will they like you? The list of "what ifs" is endless. I knew I was very good at what I did. I was sure I had life pretty much figured out at the ripe old age of twenty-four. Guess what? I discovered I still had a lot to learn! There was the never-ending need for money for supplies, books, gas, insurance, lodging, utilities, etc. I was pushing myself beyond my limits, and my body was feeling it. On top of that, my spirit was growing weary. I remember thinking that I didn't even have the strength to hold my shield of faith anymore. I was weary.

For anyone who has suffered disfigurement of any kind, it's difficult to be in a public setting. Being self-conscious is the obvious problem, but the emotional toll of being so different compounds the issue. Because I worked hard and was good at my profession, the public came to me. Still, many times I felt extremely alone and "left behind."

I encourage anyone who is facing a similar situation to remain focused on others and not yourself. Feelings are deceptive and easily manipulated by the enemy. If you're tempted to fall into self pity, counteract it with selflessness towards others. This was the only way out of the empty vacuum that I found myself in. Focusing on others gives God room to set things right in your life. He will honor you as you maintain integrity during an injustice. God quietly picks us up in our shattered state and begins a miraculous transformation, much like the way heat and pressure transform carbon into a flawless diamond.

It was during a bout with self-pity that I had my first angelic encounter. It was early one morning after everyone but Mom had left for the day, and I felt so alone. I knelt down to pray, desperate for help from God. My head was bowed, and suddenly I was lifted by my shoulders. It was as if a powerful being had grabbed me by both arms. It was a helpless feeling—my legs were dangling, and I flailed around, wondering what was happening. I was completely turned around and then set back down. It felt like the part of a roller coaster ride when you're suspended in space for a brief moment. It happened so quickly. This angel literally turned me around!

In the years following that experience, I noticed my life was changing. It was unexplainable. I had thought I was going the right way, and yet God sent an angel to set me in the right direction. One of the greatest things that happened to me between the ages of twenty-two and thirty-five was that I died to myself and my own needs, wants and hopes. (I focused on helping my siblings establish their lives and get a good college education.) Because of that, now I can do exceedingly and abundantly above what I ever hoped or asked for because my motives are pure. Reaching this state of freedom is difficult. But if you are going to be placed in any leadership role, the needs of others must come first. This is a hard lesson to learn, but crucial!

∎ ∎ ∎

It seemed as if most everything in 1986 went wrong. I really admired Astronaut Judith Reznick, who was Jewish. Judith was one of the crew who died when the Challenger spacecraft exploded on January 28, my mother's fifty-first birthday. It started my year with a lot of sadness.

I had remained in touch with Tracy, my physical therapist from the University of Iowa Burn Unit. I remember thinking Tracy was like an angel. She had instilled a unique hope in me as I worked to recover from my accident. About two years after my hospitalization, Tracy had developed lymphoma and breast cancer. I had frequently written her to encourage her and had occasionally sent her some of my wildlife pictures. Early on the morning of March 30, I had a night vision that seemed incredibly real. In the vision, Tracy came to visit and was glad to see me. Accompanying her were two huge angelic beings. They did not speak a word. I hugged Tracy. The visitation was so real that I could actually touch her and see the angelic beings that were with her. Suddenly, the two huge angels communicated to her, "It is time to go!" They didn't say a word, but somehow I was able to hear their thoughts. Then they disappeared as quickly as they had arrived.

When I awoke, I quickly ran down the stairs and rummaged through the desk, looking for paper so that I could write Tracy a letter. Mom saw that I was frantic and said, "What is the matter with you?" I hurriedly explained, "Tracy is in trouble. I need to write to her now!"

Just then the phone rang. It was Kathy, a friend and fellow burn patient who was still an outpatient at the University of Iowa Burn Unit. Mom answered the phone.

Kathy told my mother that Tracy had died during the night! She died on Easter at age thirty-one. I was so sad to lose her. She was so young and had such a wonderful life ahead of her. She visited me as she left Earth. In my vision she was so happy to meet me, hug me, and say goodbye. Even though she never spoke those words, the intention was communicated to me.

■ ■ ■

During this season of trials, change, and testing, I had yet another very real vision. I was actually taken up and out somewhere. I believe that sometime in my life journey, I will arrive at the place I saw in this vision and will recognize it. (My prayer is that the Holy Spirit would anoint the words as I share this vision, that it would empower and encourage you. I pray for supernatural wisdom and discernment to bless your life!)

The vision was so real that I could actually feel the pavement under my feet! In this vision, Jesus appeared to me! We were in a huge courtyard late in the day, and it was getting dark. Jesus was weeping mournfully on my left shoulder. I have never seen a human in such desperate grief. I understood it to be the night before He was to be crucified, and everyone but Mary Magdalene had abandoned him. I comforted Him as He leaned on me, sobbing in anguish. I desperately wanted to give Him comfort and said, "Jesus, I am going to help you!"

I am about six feet two inches tall, and he was just slightly shorter than me. I would judge His height at five feet eleven inches. In the vision He wore a hood. Mary Magdalene stood on His left side, experiencing anguish in her heart also. I was deeply affected by the magnitude of His sorrow.

In my attempt to help Jesus, I took off running. I was barefoot and could feel the warm, smooth cobblestone pavement below my feet. I was actually there! The stones were smooth and about five inches around in the huge, walled courtyard. When I woke up, I knew in my heart that I had been with the Lord. This vision changed my perspective. Jesus' being on my left side was in accordance with what we know from the Word; we are seated at His right hand in the heavenlies.

This vision also confirmed something that happened to me when I was fifteen. I had my shirt off one summer day, and my youngest sister, Joanne, said, "John, look at your left shoulder blade. There is a perfectly shaped heart on your back!"

It was difficult for me to see, due to its location. But just as my sister said, there was a perfectly shaped heart on my left shoulder. It was about three inches in diameter and looked like the outline of a scar. Amazing! Jesus was showing His love for me at that time.

■ ■ ■

During this time of restoration, my business was doing well. My mother and I decided that since all my siblings were in college at the same time, we would go also. We enrolled at an area community college, taking one class at a time. We would score almost the same on our tests. We both had a grade point average of 3.89. We studied in the morning and then I would go into the studio to work.

During this time I tried to become more serious about my career as an artist. My first wildlife print, "Golden Summer Delight," was completed in the autumn of 1992. I had sent copies of the print to Iowa Governor Terry Branstad, actress Elizabeth Taylor, and actor Gene Kelly. I received letters from all saying that they loved the print—a nice compliment for my first print. I was extremely pleased to have completed it, considering all I had been through since the accident. My journey had been an inspiration that compelled me not to give up. This was another major step in the restoration of my hope and reestablishment of my dreams.

The next year I submitted an entry for the Federal Duck Stamp Competition in Washington, D.C. This had been a dream since the age of fourteen. At first, I was pleasantly surprised to learn that I tied for sixteenth place out of 283 entries. But the excitement was temporary; I learned that the judges had erred, and I actually placed last. I wasn't deterred, though, and entered again the following year. My second attempt was a tie for eighteenth place out of 585 entries. I tied with Maynard Reece, who is the record holder as five-time winner of the competition. Quite an honor, indeed!

When God restores what was taken away, He often exalts us to a higher place than we could have ever achieved without the season of testing. I want to remind you that God will restore your life to an overflowing fullness of calmness, confidence, and peace. I have lived through some pretty hard life lessons, yet in the darkest journey of my soul God was always there directing my path. God is currently doing the same in your life, even though you may be unaware of it. He will restore what the enemy has taken from you. It only takes time and a willing heart. God will take you to heights you have never imagined. Our Abba is faithful and will restore your life in areas that you may have never thought of. He will then empower you with the wisdom to make the proper changes that will accelerate your progress and give you new, fresh insight into life itself. My friend Zev Kedem, a "Schindler Jew," once told me that he accomplished more with his life because of the Holocaust than he would have without it. The experience pushed him further toward achieving remarkable things.

■ ■ ■

Accomplishing incredible things as an artist was the beginning of a longtime dream. My mother was the quality control person when the art pieces went to the printer. I needed to have another person's perspective in the printing process.

In the spring of 1997, I was working on my fifth print. There had been so much activity and responsibility in my life. I had been helping my sister Sharon remodel her home, and Mom and I were attending Upper Iowa University. After just a few more classes, we would be in our senior year. During spring break we traveled to Lancaster, Wisconsin, to celebrate my brother Mark's ordination as a minister. A couple from the church invited us over following the ceremony to celebrate St. Patrick's Day. It was particularly special for mom because she was Irish!

That week Mom had not felt well. So on Thursday I took the day off to take care of her. She shared that Jesus' mother had visited her three times that day, saying to her, "My dear, dear daughter, it will be alright!"

Then my mother became very serious and personal as she told me, "John, I know how hard this has been on you, having to wait so long for a wife. God has a 'very special lady' picked out for you! You will be rewarded for your faithfulness to your family. You will be so glad you waited! She will be very special!" She then went on to tell me about the archangel Michael, who had visited her on numerous occasions. She described his appearance and his powerful presence. She said that he had once brought the archangel Raphael with him. Mom said that Michael was fierce but Raphael always smiled.

When I got up early the next morning, I noticed a heavenly peace in our home. When I went to check on my mother, I discovered that she had died during the night. She was sixty-two years old. I was devastated. My mother was truly a good friend to me.

God's mercy gave me the strength to get through that very difficult time. I had to call all of my siblings and give them the news. My brother Mark could not be located at first, and when he got word to call me, he expected to hear that something had happened to Dad, who had almost died the prior night and was in intensive care with an aortic aneurysm. I had to break the news to him that it was Mom who had died. Over the next three days, I contacted nearly three hundred of Mom's friends and those who had meant so much to her. Mom had been the co-founder of the Iowa Right to Life Committee, and many wanted to honor her.

I thought I had known loneliness before, but this was the first time in my life that I felt entirely alone. I had no one to share my grief with. It was a very hard time of loss, darkness, and uncertainty. I had too many people who depended on me, and it drained my energy. I was left to deal with most of the aftermath following Mom's death. There were thank you notes to be written. But I felt abandoned by God and man.

■ ■ ■

As I look back on that time in my life, I know that God was there by my side giving me energy and hope. The growth that has occurred as I have moved beyond my comfort zone has been incredible. I have many good memories. I am reminded of how my mother would smile and say, "John, it's time that I pass the torch on to you...but guess what? You're still holding it!" (She was referring to my willingness to fill in the gap for my family.)

Even in the painful moments of life, we must hold on to hope and develop deeper levels of truth, knowing that God *will* give us the tools to survive! When I faced my darkest moments of loss, it seemed there was no way out. I wondered if recovery was even possible. But in moments like those, when our strength withers like violets in a parched desert, God steps in with power to deliver His beloved children. He cradles us in the arms of love and protects us from the hideous sandstorms of life, protecting us like the pupil of His own eye.

Come into the reality that God is a great God! He will provide an avenue of miraculous rescue. Look at Moses; he was caught at the Red Sea with millions of desperate people as Pharaoh's royal army approached to crush them! Even a Hollywood writer could not have provided such a dramatic script. But God delivered them from a desperate situation, and all of the acknowledging world still talks about it. (Science has recently proven this as fact; archaeologists have discovered golden chariot wheels and horse and human bones with coral growing from them in the bottom of the Gulf of Aquaba.) So know this, precious saint, your miracle will soon be here also!

■ ■ ■

PRAYER OF ENCOURAGEMENT: Father, in Jesus name I ask that you cover those who have lost an immediate family member. It is difficult to explain the pain to someone who has not experienced it. Jesus, you understood this at the death of John the Baptist and Lazarus—your friends. I ask, Lord, that those who are mourning be covered with your love. And give wisdom to those who are helping them during this time of sadness. I ask for a holy covering of your people when the unexpected happens. Give them comfort and courage in the crisis. Amen.

CHAPTER TEN

AFTER THE RAIN, THE SUN BEGINS TO SHINE

Discovering Purpose After Tragedy

Late in the year my mother died, I received a mailing explaining how I could buy the freedom of one person, a Jew from Russia, for three hundred and fifty dollars. I thought to myself, "What a bargain!"

That's how I became involved with the International Fellowship of Christians and Jews (IFCJ). In November, I paid for one person's freedom flight from Russia to Israel. I sponsored eight airlifts the next year and twelve the year after that. In 2001 I bought freedom flights for forty-two Russian Jews to Jerusalem. I had discovered my purpose!

For seventy-four years, Russia's communist government would not allow Jews to immigrate. The Russian Jews who wanted to immigrate were called Refuzniks. The government persecuted and imprisoned simply because they wanted to go home. Many lost jobs and were blacklisted. Some survived by living in the wilderness of the Ural Mountains. During the communist years, the Jews were not considered Russian citizens, but rather were known as refugees. The most famous of the Refuzniks was

Anatoly (Natan) Shiransky, former Israeli government minister, who spent nine years as a political prisoner in a Soviet gulag before President Ronald Reagan got him released in 1982.

The Russian Jews have always been thought of as subhuman, being deprived of their property and rights. During the nineteenth and twentieth century, there was a series of bloody pogroms in which many thousands died. In 1699, the czar's wife did not like the Jews. At her order there was a forced relocation of all Jews into what is now Poland and Ukraine.

Then, in 1990, the doors of immigration opened, and the IFCJ became instrumental in fulfilling biblical prophecy. The Bible says, "He will raise a flag among the nations for them to rally to; he will gather the scattered Israelites from the ends of the earth" (Isa. 11:12). "Then my people will know I am the Lord their God—responsible for sending them away to exile, and responsible for bringing them home. I will leave none of them remaining among the nations" (Ezek. 39:28).

The Hebrew word "aliyah" means ascension or immigration to the land of Israel. In the past eighteen years, the IFCJ has made over one million immigrations to Israel possible, according to Morene Dunn at the IFCJ. In the first two years of immigration (1990-1991) two hundred thousand people made aliyah to Israel with the cooperation of multiple organizations like the IFCJ. Since my involvement with the IFCJ, I have been to Israel twice and to the former Soviet Union seven times. Each trip has been filled with divine appointments. God is always working behind the scenes to prepare blessings for His people.

When I was eight or nine years old, I had a recurring dream about rising up on the wings of eagles. I had this dream constantly. Another dream showed me that I would be involved with Israel, and I knew I would have to learn the language. When I was twelve, this was confirmed through prophetic words spoken over me and through a gift of signs and wonders.

It was only recently that I realized what those dreams meant. I almost forgot about them, but the Holy Spirit reminded me. The airlift program I am involved with is called "Wings of Eagles." I was given the vision for this even before the IFCJ existed!

■ ■ ■

In August 1998, I was upstairs working on a painting and called my prayer warrior friend, Rose Nielson. As we were praying over the phone, Rose said, "Oh my God, John! The hair is standing up on the back of my neck! There is this huge, huge angel at the head of your bed!" (Rose did not know that I was in my bedroom studio.) She then said, "John, he is so huge that his head and shoulders are stooped because of the ceiling." I knew who this angel was. I asked Rose to ask him his name. The angel told Rose, "I am the archangel Michael!"

I started to laugh, because I *knew* who he was from the description my mother had given me. She had told me that he was like a nine-foot tall bouncer! Then Rose said, "John, he has fire coming out of his eyes, and he has a shield in his left hand and a sword raised in his right hand. He is there to protect you!" Rose was so excited by this angelic visitation. She then said, "Michael is your protector, and was sent to protect you and your farm!" (I was stepping into a calling and would need protection and wisdom. I later received a death threat because of my involvement with Israel.) Then she said, "Michael has a golden garment around his waist and his hair is golden colored." This was my first encounter with Michael. Praise God! Thank you, Jesus, for sending help when we need it!

■ ■ ■

In October of that year I began having visions of what God was calling me to—a healing ministry. In the visions, I was used of the Lord Jesus and He healed everyone. There was a lot of power, and when I would raise my left hand over the crowd, people would fall backwards as if a tidal wave had swept them off their feet. This vision occurred in many forms, many times, and was always the same; it was about healing people, setting captives free, and demonstrating God's power.

In one particular vision, I was in a church service praising God with my eyes closed, hands in the air. Everyone began to laugh at me, but I didn't care. I opened my eyes and looked up. It was then that I saw ten round circles of light dancing on the ceiling. They looked like pen lights. As I wiggled my fingers, I noticed that there were shafts of light coming from my fingertips. Any movement of my fingers caused the lights to dance on the ceiling. Someone said excitedly, "John, look at your face! There is light coming from your face!" I could not see my face, but knew what they meant.

Recently I had a confirmation when out of the blue a woman in my church said, "John, like Moses, you are going to have light coming from your face!" I then told her that I had a vision about that. I have identified with Moses since I was about ten years old. God plants seeds in us for a purpose, even if we can't understand at the time.

Whenever God gives you a word, it is meant to encourage you on your journey. I had a word that changed my life on December 30, 1999. It came at a time when Rose and I were praying. "God is empowering you with great significance, with many abilities," she said. "You will have absolute assertiveness! This year, 2000, will be a year of full restoration and unity!" This word changed my life! When my mother died in 1997 I lost belief in myself. But it seemed like along with this word, God put a supernatural mantle on me. I began to walk with absolute assertiveness and was very sincere and humble in this walk.

■ ■ ■

About six weeks later, I met a very special woman. To protect her identity, I am going to change her name and occupation as I share this true story as a witness to God's faithfulness to me. I had read in the newspaper that a woman named Julia was staying in the Metro area. She was a motivational speaker and would be in the area for several weeks. I wanted to meet her, remembering that God had promised to bless me with a special lady! I called Catherine, my brother Mark's fiancée, and asked if she would go with me to meet Julia. It was five days before Julia was to leave the area, and Catherine's schedule was open.

On February 24, 2000, Catherine, my sister Sharon, and I went to hear Julia speak on "World Peace and Unity." I was in the audience and remember how nervous I was about finally having the chance to meet her. She was so attractive! I had two hours to observe her gracious manner as she gave the presentation. I noticed that from time to time she looked in my direction. As I was sitting there, I said to God, "Assign me godliness and integrity and put your light on me!" (King David said the same thing in Psalm 25).

When Julia finished her presentation, Catherine said to me, "I am going to go up and meet my new best friend!" The two of them had so much in common! I had left a message for Julia that Catherine wanted to meet her, so I think she was looking for her. When they met, Julia reached out and touched Catherine's hair and commented on how beautiful it was.

Julia was taller than I had thought from the picture in the newspaper. She was five feet nine inches and had a sweet, gentle spirit of innocence about her. As I came near her she quickly put her right arm straight out at my eye level then flipped her hand down to shake my hand, and about knocked my nose off! With a lot of enthusiasm, she then said, "Hi! I'm Julia!"

I held her hand and we talked for quite a while. In my spirit I asked God, "Is this the woman I am supposed to be looking for?" (I had a dream twelve years earlier that I would meet someone who looked like her). I then looked very closely into her eyes. They were very warm, brown, expressive, and pure. When the light hit them, they beamed like diamonds. I was so close that I was in her personal space, but this did not offend her. I wanted

to know if she was the one that God had chosen for me. I was
so close that I am sure people thought I was going to kiss her.
Then, all of a sudden, my eyes went into autofocus zoom! In my
visual field, all I could see to the left was the warm brown color
of her iris, and to the right the black of her pupil. That was the
whole scope of my vision! I was intently looking into her eyes.
It seemed like it went on for an eon. I then told her that I had to
go and see what Catherine was doing. I was kind of embarrassed,
as it was a moment in time when everything seemed to stop. I
stepped down off the stage, and Julia went to take group pictures
with the staff.

I left the auditorium and went into the front lobby. While I
was talking with Catherine, the door opened and there stood
Julia with a five-year-old child. It seemed she was coming to
check me out, and she brought the child so she didn't look
obvious! She looked at me for a few moments and then smiled
and went back into the auditorium. On the drive home I asked
Catherine, "Should I send her some roses? Three dozen or ten
dozen, it would not matter to me!" Catherine said, "Roses always
touch a lady's heart!"

The next morning, I sent her three dozen roses in a large
arrangement. At about 11 a.m. I received a call from a woman
with the most tender, warm, professional voice; it was Julia,
thanking me for the roses. I really didn't think she would call. The
first thing I said to her was, "You are such a gracious woman!"
We talked for quite some time, and then she said, "I am bowled
her over with the roses!" I told her I had no ulterior motives. She
said, "I know you don't." It was so innocent and pure. After we
hung up, I started to cry and said "God, this is the one I have
waited for, so long, the one my mother talked about."

I went to visit my brother in Wisconsin that weekend and
called Julia at the auditorium as she was preparing to give her last
presentation. I asked her when she would be going back to New
York. She told me that she would be leaving the next morning. So
I called a florist and asked them to box another three dozen fresh

roses for Julia to take with her on the plane. She was so honored. It really had a dramatic effect as she left. She was ecstatic! She told me that I made her feel like a diva. She said, "I will always remember your amazing thoughtfulness!" This was a very special time in my life. It was a time of purity and innocence. I was so in love with Julia. I felt like I had this glowing energy coming from me.

I kept in contact with her for about seven months. I told her how much God loved her and that she was so special! I was able to witness to and encourage her during this time. But we both had people in our lives who opposed the relationship from the beginning, and I eventually realized that her career would be the passion in her life.

Inspired by meeting Julia, I decided to increase my goal of airlifting Russian Jews through the International Fellowship of Christians and Jews from seven hundred to two thousand aliyahs. I did not know at the time that Julia was Jewish!

On June 6, 2000, Rose and I were praying for Julia, and the Archangel Michael appeared again. Rose said, "John, Michael is here again! The hair is standing up on my arms and the back of my neck!" Michael is fierce. He never smiles! I asked him, "What do you think of Julia?" A huge grin appeared on his face, and he said, "I am going to go to New York and protect Julia!" I didn't know what he was protecting her from. But I asked him, "What am I supposed to do?" He said, "Keep doing what you are doing." I said, "What am I doing that I am supposed to keep doing?" Michael said, "Keep sending the Jews home!"

The year 2000 brought so much restoration to my life. I had the hope of Julia. I sincerely loved her with a pure, selfless love. She knew that! I am very real, and that is what she liked about me. I thank God that I had the opportunity to meet Julia. I loved her greatly! But I came to understand that she had other responsibilities in her life. So I just told God that I greatly honored her and that I wanted him to bless her for the gift she was to me in my life for that brief time.

Fifteen months after Michael said he would be protecting Julia, I found out that she was sick and missed work, for the first time ever, the morning of September 11, 2001. You see, Julia worked in the World Trade Center! That is what Michael was talking about when he said, "I am going to go to New York and protect Julia!" I shed tears of thanksgiving when I realized this.

I knew that God would honor my integrity towards Julia and use it in finding someone else for me. This someone else would be very, very special. I would greatly honor her above anything she could think of or imagine!

In trusting God, I later met my fiancée, Victoria. After much heart ache, when I quit looking for love, God brought Victoria into my life in 2007. When I first met her, I was so pleased; we were both very comfortable around each other. The funny part is that when I quit looking—after a number of painful relationships—she actually pursued me. So this is a new chapter of the Lord's story of restoration in my life.

God *does* reward His people. Just keep believing and keep trusting God. He is always faithful! I am telling you about Julia because of the impact she had on me and also because of the angelic intervention that protected her. God will restore your life. Be patient and full of hope! Every promise that you have been given will be fulfilled!

■ ■ ■

PRAYER OF ENCOURAGEMENT: Father, I pray you give your people special, intimate times of your love. Father, give them dreams and anointed visions. Father, fill the empty places in their hearts as they go through their trials. Father, please send warring angels to protect your people. Let the ever-present help of the Holy Spirit comfort your children as they go through those trials. Let them know that they are never alone. I ask this in Jesus' name.

CHAPTER ELEVEN

ZEV KEDEM

A Schindler Jew Celebrates Life!

I was excited about the opportunity to hear a Schindler Jew, Zev Kedem speak at the University of Wisconsin, Platteville, on April 30, 2002. I took a gift for him, an original drawing I did of a ram's head. I approached the events coordinator, explaining my mission of rescuing Russian Jews and explaining that I had brought a gift for Zev. She said I could present the gift to him after the event.

A short time later, she informed me that Zev had asked to meet me and that I would be able to present the gift to him before the event. When I met Zev, I explained that the ram's head was titled "Isaac's Replacement," and he looked at it wide-eyed. He told me he was doing an in-depth Bible study of Isaac and the ram. I said, "Then this was meant to be." He told me he knew exactly where he would hang the drawing—above the mantle in his home.

I was able to speak with Zev more about my call to rescue Russian Jews. He told me, "John, what I like about you is that you take action. We are fellow survivors!" He had a fairly proper British accent, having been raised in England as a war orphan. He further explained that his four children, who live in Old Jerusalem, were unaware of his traumatic past until he shared it following the movie "Schindler's List." He was actually played by a child actor in the movie; Zev was the nine-year-old orphan who was brought to Oskar Schindler's factory. And Zev personally appears at the end of the movie in the real footage of Holocaust survivors.

We took an instant liking to each other and could have talked for hours. He grabbed me and said, "John, let's get our picture taken together!" After this, the coordinator came to tell Zev it was time to speak. As I entered the auditorium, I was startled to see it packed with people waiting to hear Zev; there was standing room only. He began his presentation, "Schindler's List: A Survivor Celebrates Life!" He talked about Oskar Schindler and his experience during the war.

Luckily, Zev was saved by Oskar Schindler, a man whose heart had been touched by God. He considers Schindler to be a Moses because he became a mighty shield and refuge for God's people during this extremely dark chapter of history in Nazi-occupied Poland. In Zev's homeland, three and a half million Polish Jews died at the brutal hands of the Nazi machine. Sadly, only four thousand Polish Jews survived. Zev was one of them.

It was Zev's mother who devised a plan that saved his life when the Nazis were exterminating people in the Krakow ghetto. They hid in a pigeon coop in their attic and heard all of the murders below in the bloody streets. Zev was there with his mother, sister and both of his grandparents. Zev's grandfather was going to take a cyanide pill and kill himself. Zev, who was five years old, started crying. This crying stopped his grandfather from taking his life. The next day, Zev's mother smuggled him into the concentration camp where she was working as a Schindler Jew. She bribed one of the soldiers to hide him under a load of valuables. (The Nazis would load whatever valuables they could find in the ghetto onto horse carts and would take them into the camp.) Zev was hidden under the pile of treasures. When he got into the camp, a doctor who was friends with his mother was waiting for him. He hid Zev for two years under his bed. It was the only place in the camp that the Nazis did not look.

As he told this story, I was sitting in the third row. The Wisconsin Legislature members and the top officials from the University of Wisconsin were right in front of me. In front of two thousand people, Zev said, "Before my presentation today, I met a man. He gave me a lovely gift. Here in your community for a few hours you have another Oskar Schindler!" It almost brought me to tears that he would compare me with the man who saved his life. I had deeply touched him, and he deeply touched me!

He then continued telling about the terrible experiences that he endured in the Nazi concentration camps. The first day he was in the camp, a group of older youth made a circle around him and walked him to the place where he worked. He was hidden from the Nazis. At this time he was only seven years old, and they killed everyone who was younger than thirteen. He worked making brushes. He would stand on a wooden crate so he looked like he was taller. Zev would out-produce the other workers because he knew his life was at stake. One morning a Nazi soldier was going to kill him. Zev's amazing mother had trained her children to speak three languages. So in perfect German, Zev cheerfully said, "Isn't this a wonderful day!" The Nazi was so disturbed that he lost it and went steaming off. He left Zev alone because he couldn't be sure Zev wasn't a German!

Zev also told a story about the little girl in the red coat in the movie. (The movie was filmed in black and white, but there are four color scenes that accentuate the story. Two of the color scenes show the flame of a single candle being lit, representing hope. At the end of the movie the surviving Schindler Jews are shown in Jerusalem paying tribute at Oskar Schindler's grave site. In the other scene, a little girl wanders the streets of Krakow as the murders are taking place. She hides in a vacant apartment under a bed. She represented innocent youth.) The little girl was actually the daughter of a judge. The day before the massacre, the judge bought her the red coat for her fifth birthday. Zev told us that the judge lived through the war, but the little girl did not; she was killed because she was a child. He said that the judge still cries and falls apart when he sees a little girl in a red coat.

There came a time when Amon Goeth, the head Nazi, was given orders to exterminate the camp. That was when Oskar Schindler paid Goeth a bribe to save his people. The trains were routed to Czechoslovakia with the Schindler Jews. But because of a clerical error in paperwork, three hundred women were rerouted to Auschwitz while the men were brought safely to Brinnlitz. Oskar Schindler was furious that the women he had paid the bribe for were taken to Auschwitz, and he went to save them. He had to bribe the head Nazi with diamonds in order to reroute the train and send the women back to his factory at Brinnlitz. Schindler had a lot of courage; this was the only time in Holocaust history that people were released from Auschwitz.

When Schindler was trying to save the women, a Nazi soldier grabbed Zev because he was young and sent him to another death camp where he became responsible for carrying dead bodies out of the infirmary. Three hundred people would die each night. At this point Oskar Schindler could not help Zev. But because God's mighty hand of protection was on Zev's life, he lived to tell his amazing story to the world.

After the war, Zev was sent to England as a war orphan. He later received a letter from his mother. She had survived the war along with his sister, but they were not allowed out of communist-occupied Poland. However, since his mother was writing to "free" England, she was considered a spy by the communists and they started monitoring her. In the last letter she was allowed to write, she told Zev to get a good education because it would serve him an entire lifetime. So Zev went to Oxford, graduating with distinction and honors. Because the communists in Poland considered his mother an enemy of the state, Zev was not allowed to see her until after the fall of communism in 1989. I can only imagine their tears of joy as they first embraced each other, having not seen each other for over forty-five years.

Zev has spoken to over two hundred universities around the world. He is a famous engineer who was responsible for rebuilding Old Jerusalem after the 1967 Yom Kippur War. He told me, "That is my work." He is also a humanitarian, philosopher, environmentalist, author, and well-known documentary film producer. (He has done four films for PBS.) He lives in Haifa and is writing his book *Love in the Holocaust,* in which he describes the sacrificial love of those who saved his life.

As he was finishing his presentation, he talked again about me, what I was doing, and what I had been through. He got emotional. I was very touched by his tenderness in telling my story of overcoming adversity! I was so blessed to have connected with him for those few moments.

Since that time, I have stayed in contact with him, and we call each other from time to time. I appreciate Zev very much. He has been a deep source of encouragement and a good friend, giving timely advice that I have listened to. Zev has such an important story to tell the world, and reaches out to university students around the world. I thank God that we met!

■ ■ ■

God will take us *wherever we are* in life and restore completely to us what injustice has taken away. Zev is such a heroic example of faith, endurance and perseverance during great loss and tragedy. What God has done with his life is truly amazing. I am here to encourage you to continue with your journey into restoration and to know that God is a loving God. He will restore your life. Your eternal, loving Father wants only the best for you. So my heartfelt wish for you is that you press into God during the dark adversity and know that He will restore you to a greater fullness.

■ ■ ■

PRAYER OF ENCOURAGEMENT: Father, in Jesus name, let your light shine forth from your people. Let them be rays of hope to a darkened world. Let them have supernatural wisdom to be in the right place at the right time, to have the right answer for those who are in need of encouragement. Father, let your people be your light, and let them be messengers of hope to people who are hurting. Let them cover and protect those who are vulnerable and give them the wisdom to make a great difference in the lives of those around them. Father, give us our divine assignments. I ask that your favor shines down on your people like a warm waterfall of love from Heaven. Let the power of your love restore and bring justice to those who have been wounded. Father, remind them by the power of the Holy Spirit that you accomplish great things in, through, and by your people. I pray this in Jesus' name and seal it with the Holy Spirit in the power of the blood of Christ. This is all possible!

CHAPTER TWELVE

DAYS OF PROMISE

The Fulfillment of a Dream

In the course of just a few months, God worked many miracles in my life. He opened doors that I could not have opened in an entire lifetime. I marvel at the restoration in my life and the fulfillment of a promise He gave me when I was twelve.

Once again the Lord appeared to me, just before my first trip to Israel. It happened to be my brother Mark's birthday, so I remember the date—October 20, 2002. I was in church, and again, Jesus was standing at my left side. But it was different than the first time; I saw His face! His complexion was fairer than I had imagined. But His eyes were the most tender, kind eyes I have ever seen. He had a look of total humility yet gentle power. I have never seen a face so pure as Jesus'. Then, in an instant He was gone, and I felt electricity and fire flash through my body, starting at my feet, then up to my head, then down to my feet again. It was like a wave of warm energy. This was the beginning of an adventure that would take me halfway around the world.

It is amazing that in the course of life, good often appears when we least expect it. The same can also be said of tragedy, of course. We often find ourselves looking into the future as if it were a foggy morning mist, yet with anticipation of the sunshine. Suddenly, the clouds of life dissipate and we understand our purpose. The human spirit understands this. We must boldly press forward with wisdom and not let fear dominate our future. I have walked in dangerous areas of the world but known that I was protected. My journey of fulfillment and discovery unfolded further with my trip to Israel and the following events.

■ ■ ■

Israel is the "Promised Land." It is the kingdom of David, the "Holy Land" of the prophets, the place of God's covenant with Abraham, the place of the fulfillment of the Messiah. But it is also the land of suicide bombings! Having survived an explosion at age nineteen, I wasn't sure if I wanted to sign up for another dangerous situation. A suicide bombing had been reported in Tel Aviv a few weeks prior to my arrival, but in my heart I knew I would be safe. There was something awaiting me, prepared in advance. I had to step into the fulfillment of my destiny.

In December 2002, my good friend Marv Pospisil and I went to Israel. We were part of a group of 435 Christians from around the world who went to Israel to intercede and show our support in her time of need. The land promised to Abraham now warmly welcomed us. We were the largest group to visit in two years.

On foot, we entered the Old City of Jerusalem, the kingdom of David (a man after God's own heart!). As I stood near King David's tomb, I realized that there were only three feet and three thousand years between us! His crypt was covered with a velvet blue cloth. He was laid behind a gate, so close that I could have actually touched the material, transcending time and history. I was amazed to be "that close" to the man who wrote the psalms, killed Goliath, conquered nations, and made so many mistakes. It was special to be in "the city of God" at that time in history!

■ ■ ■

The humanness displayed by King David has inspired us for generations. The concept that God will use everyday people to overcome incredible foes has captivated the weary traveler, strengthening him for the journey ahead. What are the "Goliaths" in your life? God used David powerfully in the restoration of Israel, fulfilling the covenant made with Abraham. In David we see ourselves, frail and prone to sin. However, David was a man after God's heart because he had the heart of a worshiper. When trouble came his way, he arose to worship.

Every generation has drawn strength from the psalms that David wrote. David failed, yes, but his heart always sought repentance and restoration in his relationship to God. We can learn much from this king whose life is portrayed in the Scriptures to teach, inspire, and correct us.

What is your response when you've received a prophetic promise and then you enter your years of testing and preparation? Growth and maturity are essential, and you can't go to school to learn it. What seems to be an obstacle will be removed in a moment once the purposes of God have been fulfilled.

It was nine long years before Samuel's prophecy would be fulfilled. The years of testing and preparation were difficult for David. This time of testing molded David's character so that when he was crowned king, God's purpose for the kingdom of Israel would be fulfilled. He was established as the king of Israel but continued to face heartache, grief and sadness during his reign. Israel grew strong as a nation under the favor of the Lord. During David's reign, worship of the Lord was established in Jerusalem. King David ruled with faith and acknowledgment of God's sovereignty, grounded in faith and the knowledge of God. David reigned in Israel from 1010 to 970 BC.

■ ■ ■

Jerusalem is an amazing city. It is the city of David and also the city of the Messiah, Jesus Christ. It is also where our Lord was crucified and bought our freedom. In Israel there is so much history to experience. We spent ten days visiting many sites, including the Church of the Holy Sepulcher. The church walls still have bullet marks from a battle that took place there during the 1967 Yom Kipper War.

Our group later visited Nazareth and then Cana, where Jesus performed His first miracle, changing water into wine. On a misty morning, we took a boat ride on the Sea of Galilee, and then went into the Golan Heights. I especially loved those mountains and the beautiful valleys and meadows. We then continued to the Mount of the Beatitudes. It was beautiful with the Sea of Galilee in the background. Our group began singing in the church, and it was a holy experience. You could feel the presence of the Lord and smell roses. We were blessed! The people of Israel are warm, friendly, and very receptive.

One of the most moving experiences for me was our visit to Yad Vashem, the memorial to the six million Jews killed in the Holocaust. Most compelling was the Children's Memorial where one million children who died are honored. It was designed with many mirrors, and it is totally dark. There are one million points of light, like stars in the night-time sky. Each light represents one child who was murdered in the Holocaust. At any time in the night when you look to the sky, your eyes can see only six thousand stars. There were one million in this memorial. It was so dark that you had to hold a hand rail to find your way out.

While at Yad Vashem, I met an attractive woman in her mid sixties. She was crying, so I went and talked with her. Her name was Marion. She told the heart-wrenching story of her grandfather, a multi-millionaire and judge in France who was gassed by the Nazis. Also she told of the abuse that her beautiful mother had endured at the hand of the brutal German SS soldiers. Marion's maternal grandparents had a secret plan of taking her into Germany, where they became Lutherans. That saved Marion's life! I told her of my efforts to rescue Russian Jews. She began to cry, saying in her sweet accent, "Dahling, when is your birthday?"

I told her, "Today!" It was very special that I could be in Israel and at Yad Vashem on my birthday.

In the "Avenue of the Righteous" I saw trees that were planted by Corrie ten Boom, Oskar Schindler and others who risked their lives saving Jews during World War II. One person's courage can save a generation! As said in the movie, *Schindler's List*, "He who saves one life, in time saves the world entire."

■ ■ ■

With a lifetime of fond memories, new friends, and renewed vitality, we sadly left Israel. The flight to New York was eleven hours. Marv and I were at the Tel Aviv airport at 1 a.m., going through the detailed Israeli Security. Little did I realize that my journey to bless Israel was only beginning.

I was standing in the shuttle, reminiscing on the events of the tour, when I saw a middle-aged, kind-looking, Orthodox Jewish man pat the seat beside him and motion for Marv to sit. In my spirit I knew that I was supposed to meet him.

It was late. We all were tired and ready to takeoff. The plane taxied, and before long we were cruising at an altitude of thirty-three thousand feet. The gentleman from the shuttle was also on our flight. At about 2 a.m., he passed by me on his way to the restroom. He gently patted me on the shoulder and smiled warmly. I felt God telling me that it was time to go and talk with him. When he came out of the restroom, I struck up a conversation. I told him that I had been airlifting Russian Jews through the IFCJ. He mentioned that he had just seen Rabbi Yechiel Eckstein, President of the IFCJ, two weeks earlier in Philadelphia. He told me that his name was Yaakov Uri and that he owned a famous pizza restaurant in Jerusalem. He then told me that he was the manager of ZAKA Rescue and Recovery. ZAKA is a Hebrew acronym for "Identification of Victims of Disaster." He explained that they are volunteer paramedics who save lives after suicide bombings in Israel. He developed the idea of putting paramedics on motorcycles. That's how they deliver hot pizza in Israel! The fully equipped "baby ambulances" can get to the scene more quickly than the larger ambulances. We talked for quite a while. Then he told me, "God just told me that you are going to be a door that opens up to me." When he said this, I was very touched and almost in tears. Yaakov is an extremely holy man. All ZAKA volunteers are holy, Orthodox Jews. We exchanged our contact information before returning to our seats. About five minutes later, he came by me, held his hand to his heart, and said, "I have feelings for you in my heart!" I told him, "It's the Holy Spirit!"

Returning home, I had great enthusiasm and a sense of renewed purpose! The very next day the phone rang; it was Yaakov. He told me that he wanted to come and visit me. I told him that I needed to get my wheels under me! So we made tentative plans for him to come in the first part of January 2003 to raise money for ZAKA to fund motorcycle units. Before he hung up the phone, he said, "I love you!" I thought to myself, *God has something really planned here! This Orthodox Jewish man considers me like his son. Wow!*

There was so much to do for my business, and the Christmas season was coming quickly. Before I realized, it was the last week in December. Yaakov called about booking his first flight into Iowa. I told him that I had arranged fifteen interviews with the press and had contacted the governor's office to see if he could meet Yaakov. I coordinated a very tight schedule for him.

It went like clockwork. As he was warmly welcomed, his friendship bonded Iowa to Israel. On the last day of his first visit, January 9, we were scheduled to speak at the Trauma Unit of St. Luke's Hospital in Cedar Rapids. Then he had a presentation at Coe College's Gage Union, where the room was packed. The Cedar Rapids Gazette sent one reporter and two photographers. There was a holy presence of God in the room as Yaakov told of the plight of ZAKA and the suicide bombings in Israel. Afterwards, I had to get him to the airport in time for his 5 p.m.

flight to New York. As he left, he hugged and kissed me and said "lehitra'ot," which in Hebrew means, "see you soon!"

■ ■ ■

As I was getting back to my business the following Monday, I received a call from the President of ZAKA, Moshe Talansky. He said that because of my work with Yaakov, they wanted to open a temporary office in Iowa and make me the chairman of the Iowa ZAKA. I was honored and I accepted. ZAKA was named the "United Nations Volunteer Organization of the year 2001!" They were on the scene after the September 11 World Trade Center bombings in New York. They have offices worldwide in Jerusalem, New York, Paris, London, Ontario, and now Iowa! He also told me that they wanted a delegation from Iowa to go to Israel and meet Prime Minister Ariel Sharon, the mayor of Jerusalem. They also wanted Iowa to be a "sister state" with Israel! I was absolutely amazed at what had transpired just because I was kind to a Jewish gentleman.

I then called Yaakov because he wanted to come back to Iowa in March. So once again I became busy working on a very detailed schedule for him. He planned on staying March 5 through March 14 because ten colleges wanted him to speak and there were forty-five interviews with the media.

At about this time, I received an interesting call from Anelia Dimitrova, the Journalism Professor at the University of Northern Iowa. Anelia has a one-hour television program that is aired worldwide called, "Here and There." She saw the interview in the Waterloo Courier and called to see if Yaakov could be a guest on her program when he came back in March. She then asked how I met him. I told her of the vision that I had of airlifting two thousand persecuted Russian Jews. When she heard this, she said that she wanted me to be on her program also. Anelia is from Bulgaria in the former Russian republic; my story touched her! The program was aired February 27, and she called it "John Dieter, Citizen of the World. Iowa's Oskar Schindler."

■ ■ ■

My second trip to Israel, in 2004, was as special as the first. I met with the mayor of Jerusalem, Uri Lupolanski. He wanted Cedar Rapids to become a "friendship city." I was the envoy.

I also had an unforgettable breakfast with Zev on the sea in Haifa. He said, "John, I think you are going to touch the world with your writing." I was greatly encouraged by him and appreciated our time together and our conversations about life and the future of Israel. He then took me to the top of Mount Caramel and showed me the beautiful gardens that cover the mountain, pointing out that Lebanon can be seen from there.

After spending time with Zev, the next day I was in Jerusalem with Yaakov. He was able to get me into the tunnel under the Temple Mount. I was amazed that I got to see the tunnel, as this was the Festival of Tabernacles holiday, and the tunnel was off limits to even the Orthodox Jews. That night he said, "John, I want to show you something you will never see anywhere in the world. So he took me into three ultra-Orthodox synagogues in Old Jerusalem. I was the only Christian in the synagogue; all eight hundred men were dressed in the Russian Orthodox outfits with the fur hats, dancing the Hag-ha-Asif dance before the Lord. So Yaakov and his son-in-law Solomon grabbed me and we danced with the other eight hundred. It was a special experience.

When we took a taxi to another synagogue, we stopped to pick up another ultra-Orthodox passenger. When he realized he was in a taxi with a Christian, he was deeply offended. He had the taxi driver stop, and he got out quickly. Yaakov told me, "Pay no attention to him." In ultra-Orthodox Jerusalem, many of the children stared at me; they had never seen a Christian before.

■ ■ ■

As I look back on the many setbacks I have survived, I also see the amazing restoration that the Lord has brought to me. Making connections around the world is a big part of that.

In addition to my trips to Israel, He has brought me to the former Soviet Union seven times. Kiev has a very long and rich history dating back fifteen hundred years. Five hundred years before it became a city, St. Peter's brother Andrew preached to the Scythians, claiming that it would be a great city of God. The Lavra monastery there is a holy site like the Vatican and Jerusalem. Coincidentally, all these cities are built on seven hills.

I stand amazed as God always prepares the path before me. When I was in Kiev in the autumn of 2006, I attended the 65th anniversary of Babi-Yar. The city of Kiev fell to the Nazis after a forty-five-day bloody battle on September 19, 1941. In a period of a few days, over one hundred thousand Jews were machine gunned into the deep trenches of Babi-Yar. Only three people survived. One was a young teenage girl named Dina Pronicheva. She fell into the pit, landing on other bodies. She was buried alive and dug her way out hours later into the dark of night. Babi-Yar is considered the largest single massacre in holocaust history. It was a remarkable experience to be in Kiev. Over sixty dignitaries from forty countries attended the event. I was very blessed to witness this high level commemoration. It reminded me to keep being a person that God can use to make a difference.

My Father God has brought me through so many trials. Everything significant in my life has God's fingerprint on it. My journey of restoration has been interesting. I share these stories to honor God for His miracles and restoration in my life.

■ ■ ■

PRAYER OF ENCOURAGEMENT: Father of light and restoration, send special messenger angels to encourage your people during their recovery. Complete the work you've begun in them more fully than they could ever imagine. Dreams, visions, light and love—Father, fill your people with your purpose for them! In Jesus' name, continue to restore them, giving them a life of enthusiasm and hope!

CHAPTER THIRTEEN

FELLOWSHIP AND FAVOR

The White House

It was amazing what restoration God was doing in my life over a very short period of time. He was fulfilling His promises and showing me His specific purposes in my life. Big doors were opening! And I was becoming increasingly connected with Israel through relationships with leaders and through helping promote ZAKA Rescue and Recovery. (There I was, a survivor of an explosion, and God was using me to help suicide bombing survivors!) I had much preparation to do for Yaakov's second trip to Iowa from Israel, scheduled for March 2003.

Coordinating Yaakov's schedule was challenging. I was dealing with officials from ten different colleges and universities in Iowa and Wisconsin as well as the mayors of Des Moines, Iowa City, Dubuque, Cedar Rapids, Ames, Cedar Falls, Waterloo, and Vinton—plus the forty-five media contacts I had made. It was difficult to coordinate everyone's schedule. But I got it done!

On Monday, March 3, I received an unexpected call from the International Fellowship of Christians and Jews. Susan Kay wanted to know if I planned to attend the "Stand for Israel" conference April 2 and 3, 2003, in Washington, D.C. Honestly, I hadn't planned on going. I had spent far too much time away from my business already. With Yaakov arriving in a few days, I didn't think I could swing it.

But Susan said, "John, do you see on the itinerary where it says, 'Briefing by invitation only'? " She continued to explain that I had been invited to the White House for a briefing on Israel. I was stunned. Middle East tensions had escalated to a point where the United States was on high alert for terrorist activity. We were preparing for war. Did I really want to be in Washington, D.C. during this volatile time? Susan explained that there were only a small number of invitations extended for this historic briefing. It took just a few brief seconds to give Susan my answer, "I will be there." So now I was trying to manage two major events at the same time!

Three days earlier I had received a call from Jerusalem. Yaakov left a message that something had come up and he would be late for the college speaking tour. It was the Sabbath and he could not be reached until the end of the Shabbat Shalom. I was nervous, wondering how much of the tour he was going to miss. The schedule was unforgiving, and this setback would be difficult.

Yaakov flew directly from Jerusalem on Friday, March 7. We had to cancel speaking engagements at the University of Iowa (Hillel Jewish Center) and Cornell College, as well as a meeting with Governor Vilsack. All I could do was cancel the events he missed and pick up when he arrived. Yaakov cannot travel after the sun goes down on the Sabbath, so I had to rush him directly to Postville for the Sabbath. We had no time to stop for anything as it was at least a two and a half hour drive from the airport. Thankfully, we made it in time and I delivered him to Rabbi Shimnel's home before turning around to make the drive home. I was grateful that there was nothing scheduled for Saturday and I could work in my studio.

I was up early Sunday morning to travel to Postville to resume Yaakov's schedule. It was extremely cold with wind chills of twenty below zero. My mission was to get him to Des Moines by noon for a meeting with the Jewish community. I had to leave home at 4:15 a.m. to get to Postville by 7 a.m. Still, I waited as Yaakov finished his morning prayers at the synagogue.

After waiting about an hour and a half, a Jeep pulled into the driveway. It was Sholom Rubashkin, the owner of a local kosher meat processing plant. He said that he had heard a lot about me and wanted to meet me. It was an honor that he would take time out of his schedule to meet me.

Soon Yaakov arrived. Sholom was excited to tell him and me that he had already raised fifteen thousand dollars, enough to buy two "baby ambulance" motorcycle units. Sholom had donated seventy-five hundred dollars, and the congregation had pooled together to give another seventy-five hundred. This small community is not particularly wealthy. It was a real blessing.

We departed, heading west toward Des Moines. We were on a poorly marked stretch of highway, and somehow I missed a turn. I found myself on a dead-end gravel road. As I backed up, trying to get back on course, I suddenly discovered I was in the ditch with the front of my car pointing towards the sky. Yaakov and I both laughed at the predicament, and he joked that we looked like a rocket ready to be launched. I was able to call for help, and the sheriff's department sent a tow truck.

In spite of the delays, we arrived in Des Moines on time. We were greeted by Rabbi Yossi Jacobson and Mark Finkelstein from the Des Moines Jewish Federation. Yaakov did three interviews, two with the Jewish newspaper and magazine called "Jewish Spark," and one with the Des Moines Register. We were also made aware of the possibility of anti-Israel protesters the next day when we visited Iowa State University in Ames. I was concerned for our safety, so I contacted my prayer warriors.

The next day we arrived at Iowa State University for Yaakov's lecture. In the audience was the area director for the Palestine

Liberation Organization (PLO). This woman had a large document briefcase, which concerned Yaakov because in Israel there are often women suicide bombers. After the presentation, she thanked Yaakov and ZAKA Rescue and Recovery for the work they were doing in Israel. ZAKA members are considered the "favorite sons of Israel" because they help everyone—Christians, Muslims and Jews.

The next day I received some news from Yaakov that his son David was having heart problems and might have to have heart surgery again. I told Yaakov that he needed to be home with his son and that I would have people pray for his healing. We had to cancel the rest of the university lecture tour and media interviews. (Family is so important; I was reminded of that as I took Yaakov to the airport. It is such a worry for a father when his child in deathly ill.) Even though Yaakov's second trip was brief, I think we accomplished a lot.

■ ■ ■

After Yaakov left, I got back to my "normal schedule" with my work in the studio. I was also preparing for the White House briefing. The purpose of the White House briefing was to reiterate the administration's policy towards Israel. It was an off-the-record briefing with many high level officials attending, and it was only two weeks away. That Wednesday, the war with Iraq began. This meant that the "Terror Alert" was at high level again, and I would be in Washington, D.C., in the middle of a war! It is so hard to travel at times like that. I wondered how safe it would be. Could Washington, D.C., have been the next target for a terrorist attack? Nobody knew. Especially not me!

I decided that I would wear a nice shirt and tie so that I didn't look like a suspect. I am tall and well-built. Usually the bigger guys get the security check first. I was surprised that I didn't even get checked in the local airport. It must have been the tie?

Tuesday afternoon, April 1, 2003, I arrived at Ronald Reagan International Airport. I took a taxi to the hotel where I would be staying. My taxi driver was an Arab gentleman and I felt cautious about saying that I was in Washington, D.C., for a forum on Israel. He had some Arab artifacts in the front of his taxi. Then I spotted a small American flag. I just smiled at him, and when we got to the hotel I gave him a nice tip, which made him smile.

After I checked in at the Royal Crown Plaza, I decided I would go for a walk to the White House since it was so close. It was about 4:30 p.m. and the temperature was wonderful. I would say it was just a perfect spring day! The cherry trees were in full bloom, as were the tulips, hyacinths and jonquils. I sat down at a park bench that was across from the White House to take it all in. There was a lot of security in front of the White House. A few war protesters had set up camp in the area. It was getting late and the sun was still up. Over all, it was a marvelous spring day in the Capitol. Surprisingly, two weeks into the war with Iraq, the atmosphere in D.C. was calm.

The next morning at the White House, I waited out on the steps, greeting people as they came. I met Billye Brim from Prayer Mountain in the Ozarks. I had seen her on television many times with Gloria Copeland. I talked with her for a while and said her ministry was responsible for my efforts with the International Fellowship of Christians and Jews and the "Wings of Eagles" program. (When I began supporting the IFCJ, I called her ministry to see if they were legitimate. I was told that they were "very legitimate" and that is when I started pursuing my vision of the airlifting of Russian Jews.)

I sat down at the briefing next to a woman named Dianne Haskett, who worked with Elizabeth Dole. She asked where I was from, and when I told her, she asked if I knew Reuven Doron. I responded that not only did I know him, but also at that time he attended my church. Reuven is a Messianic Jew, an author and speaker known around the world.

Dianne then asked about my accident. When I shared briefly about the explosion, she began to tell me about an automobile accident that severely damaged her face when she was only sixteen. She had been through numerous reconstructive surgeries, but you would never know it to look at her.

Many notable Christian leaders from around the world were in attendance. They came from Holland, England and other European countries that were strong supporters of Israel. The focus was the "Road Map" in Israel, a hot topic for Christians around the world who don't want Israel to surrender the land given them by God in His covenant with Abraham. In the Bible, the twelfth chapter of Genesis tells of God's promise to Abraham: "Leave your country, your people and your father's household and go to the land I will show you" (Gen. 12:1).

Following the briefing was a session at the Mayflower Hotel for over seven hundred people. Many well-known speakers were scheduled, including Attorney General John Ashcroft. That evening there was a congressional awards banquet. I was fortunate to be seated at a table near the honoree, Congressman Tom Lantos. I was placed at a table with Susan Kay from the IFCJ. There were over forty members of Congress there to honor Congressmen Tom Lantos (a Holocaust survivor) and Tom DeLay, two of Israel's greatest supporters.

At nearby tables I was able to identify the Ambassador to Hungary, Congressman Lantos, and Israel's Ambassador to the United States, Danny Ayalon.

After the meal, Tom Lantos spoke first and shared about his experiences during the Holocaust. He shared that it had been a Christian who saved his life. Raoul Wallenberg was a Swedish diplomat who created false passports for the Jews living in Hungary. By the spring of 1944, Hitler's army had annihilated a significant number of Jews in Europe. Only seven hundred thousand Jews remained in Budapest, Hungary. Adolph Eichmann was in charge of the plan for mass deportation of these Jews. The allied nations, as well as the neutral countries, felt the limited number of protection passes being issued were not enough. The search began for someone to travel to Hungary, the Swedish diplomatic auspices, to intervene on behalf of the Hungarian Jews.

Swedish businessman Rauol Wallenberg was appointed Secretary of the Swedish Legislation in Budapest at age thirty-two. Wallenberg had the ability to persuade and intimidate, but he had no prior diplomatic experience. By the time he arrived in Budapest on July 4, 1944, four hundred thousand Jewish men, women and children had already been deported to death camps in southern Poland. Two hundred and thirty thousand were all that remained of the Jewish population in Hungary.

During the six months that Raoul Wallenberg was in Budapest, he was responsible for the survival of one hundred thousand Jews. They would print false passports that could not be detected by the Nazis. The city was liberated by the Soviet army in January 1945. Wallenberg was arrested by the Soviets and never heard of again. There had been reports from former Soviet prisoners that Wallenberg was still alive up until 1990.

It was such a blessing to hear this story from one of the survivors. Tom Lantos shared about the importance of the Christian and Jewish communities supporting each other. Raoul Wallenberg is one of only a few people who are considered Honorary Citizens of America.

I was honored to have the opportunity to meet Congressman Lantos after the briefing. I also approached the Israeli Ambassador, Danny Ayalon, to introduce myself. I explained that I had been involved with ZAKA Rescue and Recovery in Jerusalem. He said he knew Yaakov. I shared about my mission to airlift Russian Jews. When we finished talking, Ambassador Ayalon said he wanted to come visit me!

Following the banquet, there was a private reception for special friends of the IFCJ. Rabbi Yechiel Eckstein was there with his staff. I knew many of them by name or voice as we had spoken on the phone previously.

Rabbi Eckstein is the president and founder of the International Fellowship of Christians and Jews, established in 1983. When he first began working with this group, his mother told him, "Yechiel, how can such a nice Jewish boy get involved with these Christians?" Some twenty years later, he has done much to bring understanding between Jews and Christians. The Hebrew word is "Sho-resh" which means "common root."

The "Stand for Israel" conference, White House briefing, and congressional awards banquet were all historic. It was also the IFCJ's twentieth anniversary. Through this ministry there have been over one million airlifts (aliyahs) from Russia, Ethiopia, Argentina and other areas of the world. These thousands of people have come home to Israel. It is often referred to as the "second exodus."

In May of 2003, Rabbi Yechiel traveled to Jerusalem and presented a check for two and a half million dollars to the head of the Israel Human Services. The money was donated by Christians in America specifically to help the poor in Israel.

At the private reception, I told the Rabbi I would be with them another forty years if that is what it took. He told me, "John, you are the oldest." I asked him what he meant and he said, "You have been with us the longest!" I was really surprised that I had been with them the longest; it was only six years. I have been consistent in giving to help the persecuted Russian Jews make aliyahs to Jerusalem.

So I am in a good position to be used greatly by God because He is directing my path! I am nothing on my own. I have supernatural protection from warrior angels and the God-given wisdom to follow. I will yield and be obedient in all that is required.

Hang onto the promises of God! This has been my interesting journey. However, with Israel, it is only beginning; I have recently stepped into greater realities and commitments with Israel!

■ ■ ■

We don't need to look very far for examples of people like you and me who overcame a lot and were used greatly to change history and the lives of people around them. There are many heroic examples. Remember Joseph who was sold into bleakness and the uncertain life of slavery and prison, yet one remarkable day was elevated to great heights. Moses also had much to overcome during forty years of feeling forgotten, working as a shepherd, and facing his past failures. King David is another example, with his human failings yet his humility to seek God's face and do God's will. Look also at what Zev Kedem endured, yet he maintained his love of people and life. So many people love him for his overcoming attitude and his ability to remain positive during adversity.

God is also doing great things in your life. He is writing greatness with your life story, even during your times of adversity. I encourage you in this!

■ ■ ■

PRAYER OF ENCOURAGEMENT: Father, I ask that you bless everyone who reads this book and that you reveal your specific plan to each of them. Father, encourage them on their journey towards their purpose. I also ask in humility that you help us accept life when it does not go as planned. Remind us that our trials are for a purpose. Give us the wisdom to see the bigger picture and to know that you are quietly at work on our behalf. Behind the scene you are preparing our destinies, unfolding our futures, and restoring our lives to greater fullness. Let integrity and humility always cover your people like a shield of safety. God, I ask you to cover your people with your love. Protect them in the nearness of your presence. Work mighty miracles for your people and let us all become gifts of encouragement to you, Father! Amen.